ALL ABOUT M

"THE HIPPY TRAIL" 1972

by

ALUN BUFFRY

Acknowledgements

Grateful appreciation to Ann Clark, Melissa Dawson and Lisa McKenna for help with the text. With thanks to Wikipedia which provided on-line information as read from Keith's travel book.

In loving memory of John Sullivan, Pete Roscoe and Paul Jolin.

Many thanks to Miriam, Mike, Marion, Keith Marshall, Hellmut, Diane and everyone that helped me on my incredible journey.

Cover by Matt Maguire, Candescent Press — www.candescentpress.co.uk

ALL ABOUT MY HAT

THE "HIPPY TRAIL" 1972

Alun Buffry

http://www.buffry.org.uk/allaboutmyhat.html
https://www.facebook.com/allaboutmyhat

DISTANCE IN MILES

Thessaloniki - Istanbul 352
Istanbul - Izmir 204
Izmir - Antalya 286
Antalya - Antakya by boat 300
Antakya - Aleppo 139
Aleppo - Deir el Zur 213
Deir el Zur - Baghdad 333
Baghdad - Tehran 560
Tehran - Mashhad
via Bandar Torkaman 625
Mashhad - Herat 230
Herat - Kandahar 350
Kandahar - Kabul 290
Kabul - Peshawar 140
Peshawar - Lahore 326
Lahore - Amritsar 30
Amritsar - Delhi 286
Delhi - Agra 130
Agra - Delhi 130
Delhi - Haridwar 130
Haridwar - Rishikesh 13
Rishikesh - Delhi 143
Delhi - Tehran 1580
Tehran - London flight 2736

TOTAL —
approx 11,000 miles

TIMELINE

March 24: Entered Turkey -
  Ibala, Istanbul, Afyon, Pamukkale,
  Efus,
  Antalya, Antakya, Reyhanli

April 10: Entered Syria -
  Aleppo, Deir el Zur, Al Bukamal

April 13: Entered Iraq -
  Al Qa'im, Baghdad, Khanaqin

April 18: Entered Iran -
  Qasr e Shirin, Tehran, Mashad, Taybad

April 24: Entered Afghanistan -
  Islam Qala, Herat, Kandahar, Kabul,
  Torkham

May 15: Entered Pakistan -
  Khyber Pass, Peshawar, Lahore

May 28: Entered India, Amritsar,
  Delhi, Agra, Haridwar, Rishikesh

July 20: Entered Pakistan -
  Wagha, Lahore, Rawalpindi, Islam-
  abad,
  Peshawar, Khyber Pass

July 29: Entered Afghanistan -
  Torkham, Kabul, Kandahar, Herat,
  Islam Qala

September 3: Entered Iran -
  Taybad, Mashad, Tehran

September 15: Entered UK

A GREEK BARBER SHOP

Let me introduce myself.

I am called Myhat. I was also known as Kapelomou.

I am quite an old hat. I was made decades ago. I had been passed many times to different heads, yet had seldom found one that I felt really comfortable on.

About forty years ago, everything changed. I found myself upon a head that I had a close affinity with and I found myself seeing, hearing, smelling much through this young man, Al - and even picking up on his emotions and thoughts.

I was lost then for several years, stored in a cupboard until, once again, I found myself on Al's head and now I can tell my tales.

Al and I spent some nine months together on our first trip, visiting many big cities and several small villages, in eight countries, all different, all new to myself and my new head – an adventure of a lifetime.

I sat on Al's head and witnessed all sorts of strange places and events while we travelled to India and then to the UK.

When Al arrived back in the UK, he was quite ill, having suffered from a problem called Infectious Hepatitis and also dysentery. Al went to his parent's house in Wales and then to hospital. But after he was in that hospital, I was never on his head so often.

I didn't know what was happening. Why was Al leaving me? How long was I to be here? What would become of me now? Would I get a new head? Would I get more adventures? Would I be treasured or neglected?

Then one day, Al took me out of my box and put me back on his head.

That is how I came to find myself back on Al's head. I have been on and off Al's head for about forty years and now I can tell my tales. We have done a lot of travelling over those forty years.

I had always been able to understand any language spoken and understood by whatever head I was placed on - but never been able to utter anything myself – until now! I have discovered that I can help Al remember the places we had experienced together and somehow I managed to place the idea of writing my tale for me. Anyway, that idea came upon Al and here he is, writing this for me!

As well as understanding the thoughts, memories and feelings of my head – I felt as he felt - I have been able to see through the eyes, hear through the ears and even taste through the mouth and tongue of my head – Al – and over the days developed a strange connection so that so long as Al was nearby, I could watch what was going on around him – even when not on his head!

I watched, I listened and I remembered – and that is how I come to write this story through a head called Al.

Al had travelled from a country called Britain, a place I had never been to and knew little about.

Al, through me, Kapelomou or Myhat, is writing this account in 2014, forty-two years after the events of 1972.

For my younger readers, I'll say that as Al looks back he remembers there were no mobile or cellular phones out there for the public to be able to buy: no Ipads or Ipods, no digital cameras, no microwave ovens, no 'Sat Nav'. Life was slower, sometimes maybe easier, without the 21st century rush.

In some places there were no telephones at all. And mail was often very slow. Communication was often very difficult outside of the immediate area, especially in the villages and towns of the Middle East.

And Al himself was thinner and fitter if less experienced with the world. I know he doubts whether he could make the same journey now, as he did back in 1972.

Al will tell you, I know, that he feels that apart from the differences in technology and in himself, little has changed. Some things are better, some things are worse.

In his opinion most countries in the world are being run by members of elite families, or Secret Societies or Military men. And almost all of them live lives of luxury at the expense of the people they are supposed to both rule and look after. In even the richest countries there are poor and homeless people sleeping on the streets.

So, on with my account of my first incredible journey into the unknown. It is all about Myhat.

My first meeting with Al took place outside a barber's shop in the Greek town of Thessaloniki.

— My Adventure Begins —

It was 1972. At that time, I understood the Greek language, hence my name Kapelomou that means Myhat, and I understood just a little English, but that was to change.

It seemed like months since I'd been left on the hook. I had been on the head of a local man who had come to the shop and left me there, never to come back.

During my time in the barber's shop, for long periods my vision and hearing had been impaired, but sometimes a young lad would come to the shop and place me on his head – then I could see and hear more clearly, and pick up on his thoughts and ideas to some extent. Later, of course, I realised that the lad's view of the world was very limited. Listening to the barber's shop chat, I learned about football and sport, politics and war, the rich and the poor – but I honestly considered the world to be quite small, and that everything that happened in it was within walking distance. I thought the rich were one side of the shop and the poor on the other and the shop itself was the great division. Much was still a mystery to me.

Konstantinos, the barber, occasionally gave me a rough dust off. He used to sometimes put me on his head and stand in his doorway when there was no hair to cut. I cannot say I felt appreciated.

One thing that Konstantinos often said was to have great influence on my life: he used to say "Watch, listen and remember!"

My life was to change in a big way. I watched, I listened and I remembered.

One day, sun-shining, dusty and quiet, with no hair to cut and no chins to shave, Konstantinos was standing in his shop doorway watching the street. I was on his head. He did that a lot on fine dusty days – street watching was almost a local custom and what was seen was often the topic of barber's chair chat. I could see through the open door and some way up the street.

A group of young people was walking towards the outside of the shop, chatting and laughing. Four males and one female. As they approached I saw that two of the males had long hair; I wondered if they would come into the shop to get it cut.

Three of the young men wore hats – well I cannot say they were as well made as myself, but there they were. Whilst I had been left hanging there for months, those hats were out seeing the world.

Konstantinos shouted something across the road – he was calling over one of the young men. He said to one: "I see you have no hat!" The young man said that he did not have one – and suddenly I found myself taken off my head, briefly dusted, and presented to him by Konstantinos.

The young man, whom I soon learned was called "Al" put me on his head. I saw the world through his eyes, a world I sensed was very different to my life so far, a world of mystery, strangeness and adventure. A world that Al was exploring with plenty of new experiences, new people and new ideas.

Brilliant! I had a new head.

I instantly understood the new language, English, spoken by my new head. I began to see with different eyes and understand the world in a way new to me.

The others were Keith, John and Mike and the female was called Marion. It doesn't take long to learn those things when all you can do is watch and listen. The fact that the humans did not know that I could watch and listen had the potential of being very useful to me as well as educational.

From the conversations I heard, I was to learn that they had all been students in a country called England, a city called Norwich and most had studied Chemistry. They had finished with schools and had set out to travel and explore, in a small van. At night they huddled together and by day they drove. We were, I gleamed, heading for Turkey – eastwards.

John, Mike and Al had been at a University together for three years, but before that had come from different places. John, Al knew, was from Slough and Mike from London; Al himself was from South Wales. Marion had studied Biology at the same University and Keith, the oldest of them, from Birmingham, was Marion's boyfriend. Of them all, Al regarded Keith as the only experienced traveller. He seemed much more confident than the others, although Al did not know much about him and had only known him for about a year. Al felt safe with all of them, feeling that they were honest and non-violent people like himself.

So, I found myself saying goodbye to what had been my home for several months, wondering what the future had in store for us all. Wondering how long I would be staying with my new head called Al. Wondering if he too would forget me, leave me on another hook, in some dark place maybe – or would I get to travel far?

It wasn't long before we all piled into the van – they had bought some of the local sweet 'Halva' and were saying how good it was, crumbling all over, getting in my brim. I did not care, I felt free.

We were heading for Istanbul, a large city in a country called Turkey. That evening we pulled up along the sea front near the town of Alexandroupoli. Keith read from his book that this town was an important port and the capital of the Evros region in the Thrace region of Greece.

Keith read aloud:

"It was originally called Dedeagach Dedeagatsh . The name was based on a local tradition of a wise dervish who spent much of his time in the shade of a local tree and was eventually buried beside it. Dedeagach remained the official name of the city throughout the Ottoman period, and the name used for it in the West until the establishment of the Hellenic Republic. In 1920 it was renamed Alexandroupoli in honour of King Alexander.

"Alexandroupoli is about nine miles west of the delta of the river Evros, forty miles from the border with Turkey, two hundred and fifteen miles from Thessaloniki on the newly constructed Egnatia highway."

Keith also read bits about the many wars this city had been involved in. We did not go into the city itself though, as it was getting late, so stopped and built a camp fire then everyone went to sleep.

The next morning, when Al woke up, Keith and Marion were already awake and making tea – which they all drank with milk added, unlike the Greek people I had seen. They were also cooking eggs for breakfast.

As Al was pouring himself some of this tea, along came a weathered and aged looking man with a donkey – smiling broadly, he pointed at the fire and the tea.

"I think he wants some tea," said Al, and he got up and poured another cup, adding some milk and sugar, and passed the mug to the old man.

"The old man first said thank you, then sipped the hot tea – only to spit it out shouting "Baba, baba!" Clearly, he did not like it. Then he opened his bag and pulled out a bottle of Ouzo.

I knew about ouzo, an aniseed-flavoured alcohol much liked in Greece and usually mixed with water. It's meant to be taken before meals but many people seemed to like it at any time of the day. Konstantinos had been one of them, but not on the days that he had to cut hair – people got very drunk and loud on that stuff, sometimes.

So the old chap offered the lads some ouzo. Al and Mike were the only two to try it – and both said they liked it. It had an aniseed taste and was strong is alcohol, making Al's head spin slightly – I had never experienced that before.

Later Keith read out about ouzo from his book:

"It was made originally in the 14th century by monks living in a monastery on Mount Athos. Ouzo is traditionally served with a small plate of a variety of appetizers called "mezes", usually small fresh fish, fries, olives and feta cheese. Ouzo can be described to have a similar taste to absinthe which is liquorice-like , but smoother."

We left for Turkey later that morning.

It was March 24, 1972.

Keith was telling them that sometimes on the border of this place Turkey, the guards took people off and cut their hair, so Al was saying he did not like that thought and maybe he would not even go to Turkey if he had known that before, but now they were on the way.

"Don't worry, man", said Keith, "just put your hair up inside your new hat."

"Great idea," said Al - "good job that barber gave me Myhat!"

"Yeah man, cool," said Keith.

I felt useful, wanted, even maybe loved, elated enough to almost fly off my new head; I didn't of course, I wanted to fit well and be kept. I wanted to stay with these people, they seemed like fun, lots of laughter and good conversation to listen to.

It did not take a day before we arrived at the border, near a place called Ipsala, and Al stuffed his hair up inside me with John doing the same with his own hair and hat. Marion, also with long hair, did not have to – apparently border guards did not object to long hair on females.

The guards, however, simply looked at the documents – the passports as they were called – and waved us through – no hat inspections, no hair inspections, no questions, just grins. As soon as we were through, the hair came down again.

I then learned something else new to me. I knew about money because men used to pay Konstantinos the barber back in Thessaloniki; the paper notes used to be called Drachmas and people had to work for them. It seems Drachmas were very important to people in Thessaloniki – that was how they were able to get their hair cut and get shaved.

We were standing outside a door into a building that had the words "Change Money" written on.

I now understood through Al that Drachmas were not used to buy things in this country, Turkey. They used money too, and they called their paper notes Lira. The team had to change their Drachmas into Lira and Al also changed some notes from his home country, British Pounds.

It seemed strange to me when I realised that this may have to be done in different places if the people used a different sort of money. The lads also had to pay a commission, so every time they would lose out. I wondered if haircuts cost the same in Lira, but I never found out.

We headed for Istanbul, which Al said was the 'gateway to Asia'. Apparently some of the city was in Europe, then, across a river, the rest of the city was in Asia. Sounded strange to me, but then I already knew from what I had heard, the world was often strange.

Istanbul was a massive and busy city, hosts of people, much

traffic – there were donkey carts on the roads along with cars, buses and trucks all tooting their horns. It was one of the noisiest places I had yet to visit. Fun though!

There were massive streets full of cars and buses, sounding their horns and weaving in and out of the traffic. There were tiny back-streets that looked un-swept for years. There were people of many nationalities and eating places suitable for all tastes and pockets. Then there was the souk – the market – packed full of tradesmen selling their wares to tourists mainly, from huge circular brass plates to Turkish fine carpets, and rows and rows of massive water pipes called hookahs, used for smoking scented tobacco.

My group found somewhere to stay, a place called a hotel, and Al shared a room with John and Mike whilst Keith and Marion had their own.

"Man, I just need a smoke," said Keith, "but we'll have to wait 'til tomorrow - I'm not going out looking for puff at night, not here man– we'll go to the Pudding Shop in the morning, for a smoke!"

Pudding Shop – for a smoke – sounded weird - puddings, smoke?!

The Pudding Shop turned out to be just that – a shop, an eating place, selling dozens of different types of pudding, made mostly of rice – some sweet and some savoury. So my team ate.

On the walls were small notices asking for lifts to India, to London, or to places in between. Apparently Istanbul was on the "hippy trail" and the Pudding Shop was full of long-hairs and short hairs on their travels. People talked about where they had been and what they had seen, with both pleasant and less pleasant tales of their experiences in places called Iran, Kabul, Peshawar, Pakistan, India and Nepal. Mostly they were good, but sometimes bad enough to put one off going anywhere.

I learnt that the Pudding Shop was really called the Lale Pastahanesi and had been opened in 1957 by two brothers, Idris and Namil Colpan. It was on Divanyolu Street in the Sultanahmet district of Istanbul, near the Blue Mosque. There was a great view of the Blue Mosque and the Hagia Sophia Mosque from the garden. People sat around eating and drinking, playing guitars and singing, and exchanging greetings and news – along with the occasional warnings. It seemed to be a place that attracted a wide variety of travellers. It felt good there. However, nobody was smoking hash and there was none for sale.

After we left the Pudding Shop, on foot, we had to cross a big bridge leading to Asia, across a wide river called the Bosphorus Strait. I had heard about rivers but never about the boats that floated on them, apparently made and guided by people, out for pleasure or business. It was one way to get around. I thought that if I ended in that river, I could get blown or washed away, so I clutched my head tightly. But that never happened. I stayed firmly on Al's head.

Keith said that he had read that the bridge, called the Galata Bridge, separated the European-side of Istanbul from the Asian side. He pulled out his guide book and read:

"It was constructed by Machinebau Ausburg Nürnberg on 1912, and connects the two sides of the Haliç district across the Bosphorus Strait."

There were people walking and people driving across the bridge, and even a few men fishing from it.

John and Al separated from the others and headed along a busy street filled with shops and stalls.

Suddenly, I heard the word "Hasheesh!"

It was a local man and he seemed to be offering John and Al something "to smoke." I knew that some humans smoked something called tobacco – it did not smell nice to me – and that included John and Al and the others, but this man was offering something else, trying to persuade them that they could trust him and go with him to get some but not to tell anyone and to smoke it only in the hotel. It didn't take much persuasion and John and Al were led down through some of the less busy back streets and eventually arrived at – oh no – another barber's shop! I did hope I would not be left there, forgotten again for months.

I also knew that Al and John had smoked hasheesh before.

The man told John and Al to wait inside where they sat watching the jolly barber sharpening his cut-throat razor. John and Al seemed worried and I don't blame them – but soon the man returned. They gave him some money and he gave them some hasheesh. "Keep it in your pocket, there are police about. Just smoke in hotel," he said. "I wonder if Keith scored," said John; I wondered if Keith was off playing some sort of game. I had heard about football.

John and Al went back to the hotel and it was not long before there was a knock on the door which seemed to cause some panic. "Open the window." said Al. "You lean out and I'll open the door and if it's cops, you sling it."

It was Keith and Mike with Marion. "Any joy man?" asked Keith.

"Yes," said John, "look what we got."

John showed the others the small lump of greenish brown hasheesh.

"Aw man, that smells ace" said Keith. "Let's barricade the door and have a joint."

A joint was made by licking and sticking some small, thin sheets of paper together – they called them "skins" – and using them to roll around a mixture of tobacco and hasheesh. A small piece of rolled-cardboard, called a roach, was inserted into one end. It was then sucked at from that end, by one of the people and lit at the other with a match. In that way they inhaled the smoke of the burning mix and then passed the joint to somebody else.

As this procedure continued, it seemed like everyone started to relax and chuckle. To be honest, I was thinking I would gain something like that from the smoke too, but smoking is not for hats – you know, no mouth, no lungs!

It was a while later that there was another knock on the door which was barricaded again, and everyone sat upright – Keith jumped up and moved over to the open window, whilst Mike went to the door and asked who it was.

"Your friend from barbers," said a voice, "I bring you coca-cola."

A short conversation and the group decided to open the door, so Mike and Al moved the furniture away from it and let in the visitor. Al said he recognised him and the man entered and placed a few bottles of drink on the floor – I had seen people drinking that whilst hanging from my hook in Thessaloniki. Some humans seemed to drink a lot but others did not like it at all. Bottles were passed around, the visitor first opening them – with his teeth. It was called cola.

He told the group that he also had some hasheesh and would roll some joints.

His way of rolling these joints was different – he made a mix of tobacco, hasheesh and opium and emptied it into some papers he had put together and placed on the floor. The others had put the tobacco in first then added the hasheesh. But the ritual of passing the joint was the same – but the smell was quite different – it was sweeter. The man said it was opium. So they carried on smoking and drinking until suddenly Al jumped up and ran out of the room.

He ran straight to the toilet – with me still on his head.

The toilet was a hole in the floor and above the hole was a shower for washing. As Al vomited down the hole, water dripped all over me – and I made sure some ran down the back of his neck too. He seemed to be trying to hold himself up between the walls!

It all ended well though. Al seemed to recover and the visitor left in high spirits and everyone breathed a sigh of relief.

There were now four men and one woman in the party, smoking hasheesh whenever they had the chance, wandering the streets of Istanbul, visiting the markets and eating houses. Then they decided to leave and head down into Turkey and maybe beyond.

With all the warning about hasheesh in Istanbul they were glad to be leaving – heading south.

The task of driving was shared between Keith and John and they were heading for a place called Afyon or Afyonkaraishar, which, Keith explained, meant "The Black Fortress of Opium". Keith added "I heard they make some great Turkish Delight there too, man, let's see if we can get some!"

Unfortunately though, it was evening by the time we arrived, so no sweets were on sale – and most eating places were closed. There were very few people on the streets.

We walked along a street with covered arcades either side and saw one man, alone, walking towards us. As he came closer, he smiled, and Keith said "Hasheesh?"

The man ran away across the road, saying "No! No! No!"

Yet, as we continued down the street, the man was following us on the other side of the road, darting from pillar to pillar. Then he came over to us again. He said if we wanted hasheesh, he could get some. We would have to drive around the town, drop him somewhere and pick him up ten minutes later. Keith agreed.

Keith drove him round the same route twice and then stopped so he could get out. "I will be back in ten minutes," said the man.

So Keith drove round the same route at least three times before we spotted the man and picked him up. "Quick!", said the man, "Drive out of town," pointing the way we were already heading.

About five minutes later he told us to turn off onto a track and stop besides the dirt road – we could see the town on one side and a small settlement of ramshackle buildings and tents on the other. The man said "I have hasheesh, but only to smoke, not to buy," and made some joints.

There under a beautiful clear and moonlit sky, he insisted that they all smoke "my way" - "inhale deeply through your hand, throw back your head and blow the smoke at the moon." This produced fits of giggles and I ended up on the ground!

Some time later, we parted company with the man, who never gave his name, and Keith asked which way to our road South. He pointed up the dirt track, telling us to turn right at the end - and off we went, with Keith driving again. I was in the other front seat, on Al's head.

After a short while the track became a road and we sped onwards. There was a turning to our right and Keith took it. Suddenly, we screeched to a halt.

It was a Turkish army camp and the two soldiers on the gates suddenly took down their rifles and pointed them at us, just as we came to a. halt. Keith shouted something to them and they relaxed and pointed us back the way from which we had just driven.

"Man, we must have fucked up and missed the turning," said Keith.

"And I'm glad we missed the bullets too," said Al. "I thought we were going to get shot, did you see their eyes?"

On we drove then, into the night. They were looking for somewhere to sleep. Keith suddenly pulled off the road, drove down a dirt track – as if he knew where he was going – and pulled up. This was where we were to spend the night, in an open area close to a shallow river. The lads set about building a camp fire.

Almost as soon as the fire was burning, we were visited by a group of young Turks, few of whom spoke any English, which was the language of my head. They had brought with them some bottles of alcohol and offered them around. Despite the lack of communication on a verbal level, there was much laughter. I sensed, however, some trepidation in my head.

The Turks were piling massive pieces of wood onto the fire which was burning away brightly and hotly – it was quite large. I heard Keith saying that he thought they needed to be told to stop, but there were now over a dozen of them. Slowly my travelling group was getting into their van saying they were going to sleep. Keith and Al went over to the group and told them we wanted to sleep now and asked that they keep the fire low and not to make too much noise. With that there were handshakes and "bye-byes" and they started to leave in groups of three or four. There were just two left, one of whom spoke English.

He walked over to the van where Keith and Al were sitting on the ground, and said "You want smoke some hasheesh?"

"Oh yeah man, you bet we do," said Keith – and once again I saw joints being rolled and smoked. The feeling of relaxation once again come into my head – and then the two Turks said goodbye and left.

I think my group was glad as there had been no trouble - we had already had rifles pointed at us by the Turkish army earlier that night!

The following morning my group was awoken by rumbling noises and shouting. As Al and the others sat up, I could see what looked like military tanks rumbling towards the small stream that was near-by. I knew about tanks as there had been pictures on the walls in Constantinos' barber's shop in Thessaloniki and the customers there talked about them and the "army" and the "war". Tanks were meant to fire at people and buildings and other tanks, with the object of destroying them. It didn't make sense to me – why would people want to kill other people – surely not fighting over hats?

Then I could see that the tanks were just part of a long convoy of military vehicles and that some of the leading ones had been driven into the river and seemed to be stuck – hence the shouting. My group started laughing – it did look odd, with two vehicles half way across the small river and all the men running round shouting, trying to push and pull them to get them to move again. The tanks were just sitting there. I wondered whether they would just shoot at the other vehicles and blow them up and get them out of the way – or would they turn and fire on us! What a start to another day in Turkey!

A couple of the soldiers walked over to us and started speaking in Turkish but when they realised we did not understand them, they just shook hands and left. A while later the convoy was able to move on.

I liked that sort of adventure as it was exciting and different, then turned out to be OK.The group ate breakfast and with John now driving, set off for the next place.

It was some hours before we reached Pamukkale Hierapolis. Mike was reading a book and said:

"This place is named after Hiera, the wife of Telephos, founder of Pergamun, in mythology.

"Here there are spectacular vast white scallop-shaped basins of water which looks like ice and frozen waterfalls, on the side of the cliffs.

"Also thermal pools with water passing though at the rate of 400 litres a second.

"It's been used since Roman times."

"Let's go take a look," said Al.

"Yes, maybe we can swim in the mineral pools, that'll be cool," said Keith.

So my group headed up the hill, stopping to look at these beautiful pools of water in their white basins. Higher up the hill we could see a hotel!

"I bet the warm pools are in there!" said Mike, pointing to the hotel.

"We'll have to sneak in, man," said Keith. The party blatantly walked into the hotel grounds and headed for the pool – there was nobody else to be seen anyway.

The sign on the front gate said 'Hotel guests only" - I suppose we were guests then.

So that's what we did. It was more of a blatant stroll than a sneak and we were inside the hotel grounds sitting besides a pool of steaming water where we could see what looked like broken statues at the bottom. "Look," said Marion, "I bet they're Roman – I am going in for a swim."

Marion jumped in - "It's lovely and warm, warmer in here than out there," she said. Keith followed her into the pool but Al, John and Mike sat on the side watching.

That evening the group drove just outside of the town and stopped to camp by the side of the road. A few joints and they were all asleep. About the only time I left Al's head was when he was sleeping.

It was in the smaller towns and villages that we passed though that I began to notice how differently the people were dressed compared to those in Thessaloniki – although I saw few women there.

Marion was dressed very differently to most of the women I had seen and very different to the women in Turkey. She, like many European and American girls I had seen at the Pudding Shop in Istanbul, wore trousers that they called jeans, but in Greece many of the women wore black skirts and tops and were covered to their feet. Now, in Turkey, all the women wore black and it seemed that the more remote the village was, the more they covered themselves up. The men too, dressed very differently to the men I had seen in Greece, and many of the children wore little more than rags, often bare-footed. It was obvious that Turkey, outside of the big cities, was populated by people poorer than in Greece.

I had gleamed from conversation, that most Turkish people were members of a religion called Islam, which was quite strict on daily prayers – they had to pray five times a day – on dress code and on diet; they did not eat pork or pig products, believing it to be unclean. I did not see the lads or Marion eat much meat at all, and I knew that Al was a vegetarian.

The topics of conversation that I had witnessed in Greece were mostly football, weather or politics. The lads and Marion did not seem interested in either football or politics – they seemed more interested in travel, music and laughter.

Whenever we stopped in a small village we were almost immediately surrounded by people, especially children, that just stood and smiled, staring at us as if in disbelief. To tell the truth I felt that they would each have liked to have had me on their head. The people were friendly enough, usually bringing somebody to us, such as the village schoolteacher who spoke English.

In one such village we were invited to play seven-a-side football, a game that seemed to be about kicking the ball around and trying to get it into a net that was guarded by a goalkeeper. Whilst the five in my party was joined by two local lads, on one side, the other team consisted of four young men, one old man and two children. They won.

Keith read from his travel guide:

"Efus, also called Ephesus, is an ancient Greek City now part of Turkey. Later it was a major Roman city on the west coast of Asia Minor, near present-day Selçuk, Izmir Province, Turkey. It was one of the twelve cities of the Ionian League during the Classical Greek era. In the Roman period, Efus had a population of more than a quarter of a million in the 1st century BC, which also made it one of the largest cities in the Mediterranean world."

"The city was famed for the Temple of Artemis, completed around 550 BC, one of the Seven Wonders of the Ancient World. Emperor Constantine the First rebuilt much of the city and erected "Efus was one of the seven churches of Asia that are cited in the Book of Revelation. The Gospel of John may have been written here. The city was the site of several fifth century Christian Councils of Efus. It is also the site of a large gladiators' graveyard.

"Today's archaeological site lies about two miles South-West of the town of Selçuk, in the Selçuk district of Izmir Province, Turkey. The ruins of Ephesus are a favourite international and local tourist attraction."

"Sounds fascinating," said John, "let's go there!"

"Oh yes, let's", said Marion enthusiastically.

"It also said that they think it is where Cleopatra had her sister

Arsinoe killed and she may be buried there," said Keith. So, this time John driving, they packed the van and set off southwards.

Upon arrival, we drove directly to the ruins. It was quite a large are by the looks of it, and it would take some time looking around.

After walking down what looked like a wide street, called the "Avenue of Heroes" with broken columns and statues on either side, grass growing through the cracks on the road, we arrived at the amphitheatre – which was quite well preserved with intact seating tiered in a semi-circle. The lads went down to the bottom area where the performers must have entertained many spectators.

John and Al started to shout lines from poems and then perform a spontaneous play as if they were ancient Greeks. I don't know what it all meant but from what I picked up from Al's head, neither did he – but I sensed they were having fun.

It only lasted about ten minutes before they started swinging their arms as if fighting with swords, and John fell to the ground as it hurt. Al also fell to the ground and the two of them were rolling round, laughing!

Suddenly there was clapping and shouts of "Encore!" – not from Keith and Mike but from a small group of what looked like tourists that had entered and were seated at the top row. I don't know whether they thought it was some sort of scheduled entertainment but they had seemingly enjoyed it. Al felt a little embarrassed, I sensed that, but all ended in good humour.

We spent the rest of the afternoon hanging out amongst the ruins, not knowing what was what. Keith said he was surprised there were no locals standing round looking to earn baksheesh by showing tourists around. It was a pleasant day and I sensed great relaxation in Al. I was happy to be on his head!

That night the party slept under the stars and then we knew that it was time for Marion to start heading back to her own country – England. She was to fly to Istanbul and then go home by train. That was when I first learnt that people could fly, although I didn't

25

know how. It was only later that I realised they needed a machine called an aeroplane to enable them to fly and it took oil to fuel it. I had never even heard about flight before that, except with birds of course. We were all sad to see Marion leave. Although I had never been on her head, I had felt I knew and liked her.

After Marion had left, we drove down to the southern coast of Turkey to Antalya and headed for a quiet beach where we were to spend the night. There was a friendly fisherman called Mustafa living in a small hut with his son, Zafer, and he invited us inside for tea. Mustafa spoke a little English and Keith asked him if he had any hasheesh. Very quietly the man said yes but he did not want his son to know. After sending the Zafer out on some short errand, Mustafa gave Keith a small piece of greenish hash. Mustafa also cooked the team some fish he had caught that day and told us that the next day he would take one of us to his village to meet his family. Also we could get some more hasheesh. Keith volunteered.

The party slept on the beach that night but in the early hours of daylight we were abruptly woken by a small group of angry looking Turkish policemen pointing guns at us and shouting. That was one of the few times that I felt Al panic – not knowing what they were shouting – but our new friend Mustafa soon came over and told us that the police wanted to see the passports and everyone, except me, had a passport – hats don't need them. The fisherman spoke to the police and then told us it was OK, he had told them we were his guests. The police started smiling and left. I sensed great relief in Al.

Later Keith went with Mustafa and Zafer and was gone for some time before returning with a big smile on his face and some more "smoke". We spent the day and evening on the beach, smoking and enjoying the warm sun. I was pleased that my brim provided shade for Al's eyes so he kept me on.

We were just outside the city and port of Antalya, the biggest place I had been to since Istanbul. It was a busy place, full of traffic, and along the port, many fishing boats of various sizes. I did not feel that Al liked it very much there.

Keith announced that he was going to catch a boat to the East of Turkey and anyone who wanted to go with him was welcome. John said that somebody would have to stay with the van and it was going to have to be him. Mike and Al decided to "toss for it" and Mike tossed a coin into the air – Al shouted out "heads" and as the coin landed on the ground, Mike said "You win!" So it was agreed that Keith and Al would buy tickets and go by boat and that the four would meet up again in six weeks, back in Istanbul. Keith went off to buy the tickets – I now sensed that both Keith and Al had very little of that stuff called money: Al said he had just twenty pounds and that they would have to live on their wits. With no van or car of their own to travel in, they would have to hitch-hike. Keith came back with two tickets and said he was going to Beirut but the problem was, he said, pointing at a ship some distance out in the water – the ship we needed to catch – but the weather was too rough for it to come all the way into port. "No problem, man" said Keith, "I'm going to ask one of those fishing boats to take us out."

Well, the sea was indeed so choppy that Keith had to ask quite a few fishermen before he found one willing to take him and Al out to the ship.

Al had already packed his rucksack and also had a sleeping bag to carry. He kept me on his head. They said goodbye to John and Mike and climbed aboard the small boat. It was up and down in the water and I sensed that Al was not too happy about this: "I can't swim", he told Keith. The wind was blowing and as Al clung on tightly to the boat, I clung on tightly to Al's head. I knew that if the wind took me away now I would be taken far away out into all that water.

When we reached the ship, I felt Al's mood drop even lower and I realised that he and Keith would have to climb a ladder a long way up to board the ship. With both boat and ship going up and down in the water, I knew that Al did not feel it was easy to do, especially with his rucksack on his back and clutching his sleeping bag in his arms. I knew that Al had some experience climbing as he had spoken to the others about his adventures rock-climbing, fell walking and caving whilst at University, so I thought he'd make

27

it up that ladder and I'd be OK so long as the wind did not catch me. Suddenly we were at the top and being helped aboard by a smiling crew. That was the first time I had ever been on a boat or on a ship.

Keith said that it was an overnight journey to the Eastern part of Turkey to a place called Iskenderun, but they didn't have a cabin and so it was very cheap – the problem was, he said, that they had very little Turkish money between them for food, and not much other money either.

The journey was very pleasant but both Keith and Al were hungry so Keith said he would try asking some of the other passengers for some money to buy dinner. A short while later Keith came back and said he's asked a crew member and "he said we can go down and finish off what's left on the table after the crew has eaten – for free." I did not feel that Al relished the thought of what he called left-overs, but when we were called and went down to the eating area we found a long table covered with many different foods: fish, chicken and meats, vegetables, cheeses, fruits, breads, sweet cakes and the cook came out and said to eat whatever we wanted and take as much as we needed in our bags. What a feast! Of course Al did not eat the meats but he ate fish and many other tasty foods and I felt his mood improve.

Also during the journey Al and Keith met some other travellers from somewhere called America and were chatting. Keith told them we were going to Beirut in Lebanon but the new friends said "It's terrible there, not at all worth visiting, we had a horrid time and glad to be out of it."

So Keith and Al chatted together and decided that instead of going to Beirut, they would head for Baghdad in Iraq. They would try to get lifts in cars or trucks, due to lack of money, but they could always catch a bus if necessary.

The next day the ship arrived in Iskenderun. Al had never even heard of this place before, so Keith read from his guidebook.

"Iskenderun is a city and urban district in the province of Hatay on the Mediterranean coast of Turkey.

The guidebook suggested that we explore the 'cave church' in which Saint Peter had preached to the Christian population of Antioch.

"Antakya, the biblical Antioch, is situated on the Asi River in a fertile surrounding. A little outside the city is the holy site where St. Peter's Grotto is situated. The cave church is the place where St. Peter preached and founded the Christian community.

"This cave is widely believed to have been dug by the Apostle Peter himself as a place for the early Christian community of Antioch to meet, and thus to be the very first Christian church. Whether or not this is so, St. Peter (and St. Paul) did preach in Antioch around 50 AD and a church had been established in Antioch by as early as 40 AD.

"The Church of Saint Peter near Antakya, Antioch,, Turkey, is composed of a cave carved into the mountainside on Mount Starius. This cave, which was used by early Christians in the Antakya region, is one of Christianity's oldest churches.

"The interior of the grotto church is austere and simple. The only permanent furnishings are a small altar, a single statue, and a stone throne. On the walls are the barely discernible remains of frescoes, and on the floor can be seen some traces of mosaics. In the back of the church is a tunnel that leads into the mountain interior, popularly believed to be a means of escape in times of persecution."

I could feel that Al was quite excited at the prospect of seeing these caves. He said to Keith: "Let's sleep here the night and see if we can get a lift to those caves in Antakya tomorrow." Keith closed his book and said "It's not far is it?"

So the two headed for the beach to sleep, but after they arrived it was not long before they were approached by a couple of local people. They chatted together in English and Keith explained that we wanted to see St Peter's first Church, the caves. Before long we were offered a lift there and off we went. We reached Antakya in the late afternoon being dropped off near the caves.

As Al and Keith walked up to the cave, we could see that there were other small caves in the hillside.

"We can sleep in one of those," said Keith, pointing, "We may have to pay to see St Peters' place but at least we'll get a free room!"

The cave of St Peter was about to be closed for the night but we did manage to go inside for a brief look. There was an English-speaking caretaker who explained that the caves had secret exit routes built in so that the monks inside could escape to safety if the caves were attacked. He told us that the cave was the first Christian Church outside the Holy Land – wherever that was, I did not know, but I sensed that Al did. There was not much else to see except what the man said was an old altar.

Keith asked him about the other caves nearby and the caretaker said they were empty, so the two climbed the slope and found a cave that had a good view of the valley and then they built a small camp fire and made a hot drink and ate some food just as it was becoming dark.

Suddenly we were approached by a group of Turkish boys, five or six of them, all shouting "hello Mister, what is your name?" and "where you come from?" They were a jolly bunch and laughed when Al told them his name. "Are you Al-lah?" said one of the boys, and the others fell about. "No," said Al, "just Al." "Peace for you," said the boy.

Another boy asked "What you do here?" and Al explained that they were going to sleep for the night."

"No, no," said the boy, "bandits will see fire and come down and rob you – you must put fire out now!"

All the boys suddenly started throwing earth onto the small fire until it was out, making big clouds of smoke in the process, and enough noise to attract St Peter let alone the bandits. Then, as fast as they had arrived, they all left, leaving Al and Keith alone in the cave and within minutes it was pitch black.

"May as well sleep and make an early start tomorrow," said Al, which is what they did. Al put me on the ground near his head and within a short while, was snoring loudly – it seemed to echo up and down the alley. I could feel that Keith was moving about restlessly for some time. Then Keith jumped up and shook Al as though to wake him.

"There's somebody out there, fuck it man" said Keith, "climbing up the slope."

Al jumped up and put me on his head. I sensed his trepidation as he began to strain his eyes peering into the darkness, where nothing could be seen. Every now and then we could hear the movement of small rocks and rubble, as if somebody was slowly creeping towards us. Al tried to peer into the blackness of the night but could see nothing but the outline of the hill opposite us and a few dim lights in the distance down the valley.

Al stayed like that for what seemed like hours, staring and listening. Nothing happened until suddenly he heard Keith snoring! He had gone to sleep. Was it all a ruse to wake Al up and stop him snoring? Al himself climbed back inside his own sleeping bag and lay there listening for hours, unable to sleep, until it started to get light again when he finally dozed off. Keith, it seemed, had slept soundly.

When Al awoke, Keith had already made tea to drink and warmed some bread by the new camp fire. "Sorry about that, Al," said Keith, "I just couldn't get to sleep while you were making so much noise snoring!"

"So were you," said Al, "I think those goats down there thought you were making a mating call to them. They were heading our way.

"At least there were no bandits!"

It wasn't long before the two men were scrambling back down the slope from the cave and standing besides the road waving their hands to try to get a lift. They had looked at the map in the guidebook and could see it was a long way to Baghdad and they would have to cross Syria first. Quite soon they were offered a lift all the way to the Turkey-Syria border.

Aleppo was just one hundred and forty miles from Antakya.

When we reached the town of Silvegozu near the border crossing, we discovered that we would have to walk through the Turkish customs and passport control, then walk about three miles through "no-man's land", to reach the Syrian customs and passport control. We also had to change some of our money into Syrian money. We did not have much in terms of British money, I knew, but I sensed that both Al and Keith were pleased that it was worth a lot more in these countries.

Al was carrying his rucksack and I had myself a great view from the top of his head. I could see we were following a rough road with fields and hills on either side. There were people working in the fields and also some animals. There was no traffic on the road at all, until suddenly a small camper van appeared. It pulled up beside the two men and the driver learned out and said hello, in English.

"Hi, where you from, where you going?" asked the driver.

"Hello, we're from England and we're on our way to Baghdad," said Al, "but we've got to get across Syria first."

"Well we're driving to Aleppo, then back, we're Aussies, good luck!"

"Any chance of a lift to the border?" asked Keith.

"Nope, sorry, we don't give lifts!" answered the driver.

"Well any chance of some water?" asked Keith – I knew both he and Al were thirsty as it was very hot.

"OK," said the driver, pouring two cups and handing one to each. "Sorry we don't have much left either."

Keith and Al drank the water and gave back the cups, and without another word the "Aussies" drove off. "Man, I hope they're not typical fucking Aussies," said Keith, "they could have fitted us in."

So on we walked and after about an hour we had reached the Syrian border post, completed formalities, bought a three-day visa, changed money- Turkish Lira into Syrian Pounds - and quickly found a lift in a truck going to Aleppo. Even though the truck driver spoke no English and neither Keith nor Al spoke his language he seemed far more friendly than the "Aussies".

It was April 10, 1972. They had three days to hitch-hike across Syria to reach the Iraq border before their visa expired.

Aleppo did not seem to interest either Al or Keith and after a night in a cheap hostel dormitory and bread, fruit and black tea for breakfast, we were soon back on the road and then inside another truck going close to our next destination, Deir el Zur. Again the driver spoke no English. Keith said that the second most-widely spoken language here was German. Al said he had studied German in school but not been very interested and had failed the exam. Keith read from the Guide Book:

"Deir el Zur — is a booming oil town in Eastern Syria on the Euphrates River. A few worthwhile attractions and the friendliness of the locals welcome those willing to go off the beaten track.

"While there may not be much in the way of tourist attractions, Deir el Zur stands out for me and other travellers I've talked to mostly because of its people."

The following day, Al and Keith hitch-hiked from Aleppo to Deir el Zur, a distance of two hundred and thirteen miles. It was quite a long time before the duo arrived in the city of Deir el Zur and found a small hotel.

To get inside they had to climb three broken steps. The room was small but cosy and Al could see the sign of a large hotel from the window, obviously much more pricey – the Hotel Continental. The hotel we were now in did not seem to have a name, just a small wooden sign saying "Hotel".

We also noticed that now most of the women were wearing black and covered their heads, some even their eyes, and almost all the men were dressed in typical Arab style gowns called Djellabas, of different colours. Some wore head scarves or turbans and most wore sandals. On the streets were stalls selling snacks such as falafels in bread, nuts and sweet cakes, others selling meat hanging from hooks, and fruits and vegetables. It was also much cleaner than most cities and for sure, people were smiling.

This was the last day of their Visa to cross Syria and Keith explained that they would have to leave early afternoon to try to get a lift to the border. If they were late they may have to pay a fine and they did not have enough money to do that. They could, however, take a stroll around the area near the hotel.

So after a cup of tea, the two decided to go out for a stroll, walking the streets just looking at the people. But it was not long before Keith said he wanted to go back to "get some kip," and Al decided to stroll around on his own. He suddenly found the Tourist Office next to a small park. He went inside the tourist office only to find that the staff spoke no English and after trying a conversation in German he picked up a map and left. He strolled into the park and sat on a wooden bench to look at the map of the town.

It was only minutes before he was approached by a couple that said "Hi!" and he knew straight away that they were Americans. They seemed friendly enough and after a couple of minutes the guy produced a small "joint". "Want to smoke some Turkish hash?"

Of course, Al wanted to do just that. So they all sat about chatting and smoking the joint – I could sense that Al found the joint very strong. After about twenty minutes the Americans left and Al decided it was time to head back to his hotel. But where was it? He did not remember it having a name or the name of the street it was on – all he could remember was that it had some broken steps in front of the entrance.

So Al headed off up a street opposite the Tourist Office – at least, he muttered to himself, if it was the wrong street he could turn round and find the Tourist Office again.

It was the wrong street! Al did turn around and tried another street, then another street – he was stoned and lost!

Now he was back at the Tourist Office for the third time at least. He sat outside to rest and think and was then approached by a young Syrian man who said "Excuse me Sir, I think you are lost – I have seen you coming back here – can I help?"

Al thanked him and said he could not remember where his small hotel was or the name – but that from the window he could see the sign for a larger hotel called 'The Continental.'

The Syrian man, who said his name was Mohammed, said he knew where that was and headed off chatting, with Al following. Suddenly in the distance, Al could see the sign and then, just as suddenly, he spotted an elderly Syrian man waving from an upstairs window. Al's eyes fell to the entrance, spotted the broken steps and the small 'hotel' sign and exclaimed, "That's it!" I felt he was relieved.

As soon as Al reached the room, Keith said, "Come on, we're late, I've arranged a lift to Iraq! They're going all the way to Baghdad. Where the heck you been anyway?"

"I got stoned and then got lost and couldn't remember where the hotel was or what it was called. I was walking up and down from the Tourist Office anyway, then I remembered the Continental sign and a guy offered help – I only knew it was our hotel 'cos of the broken step."

"Anyway man," said Keith laughing, "stoned or not we gotta go."

They had to walk to the outskirts of the City where there would be a convoy of trucks arranged by the hotel manager, waiting to pick them up and take them towards the border. That was no problem. The trucks were waiting and eagerly set off, with Al in one truck and Keith in another, about five trucks in all. The driver of our truck spoke no English and very few words of German, so Al settled down to try to read. The countryside was very brown and hilly, very dry looking but quite beautiful. Then Al tried to ask what time they would reach Baghdad. Al pointed to his watch.

The man held up three fingers and Al became confused. They could not possibly reach Baghdad in three hours.

So after trying a few words in German, Al realised it would not take three hours but three days! He had to try to explain that they only had about eight hours to get to the border and out of Syrian because their Visas would expire – and he had no way of contacting Keith.

Al managed to explain and found out that it would be over three days before they reached the border and that they were heading for Baghdad via a place called Mosul – they were in fact, back on the road going towards Aleppo.

A short while later, the driver pulled into an area by the side of the road where other trucks were parked, and our convoy stopped for a break. The break consisted of bread, fruit and meat, and a drink called "Ouzo", an anise-flavoured alcohol that I had become familiar to me back in Konstantino's barber shop. Al explained to Keith that they had a problem and were heading the wrong way and on a much longer route to the border. Somehow, he explained, much to Keith's surprise as he was oblivious to the problem, having been asleep, they would have to get back into Deir el Zur and find a lift to the border but it was now late afternoon and they had just eight hours to get there. "Doesn't look good," said Keith.

Al's friendly truck driver came over with another driver who spoke some English and after the problem was explained the man said "No Problem, I take you to truck stop in Deir el Zur then I find you good lift right way! But first we drink!"

They did not seem to worry about drink driving in Syria – at least these truck drivers didn't - and before long, Al and Keith had both drank enough Ouzo and water mix to start laughing and staggering slightly. It was going to be an interesting evening getting to Iraq.

True to his word, the driver introduced Keith and Al to the new driver and they climbed aboard and soon they had passed through Deir el Zur. They pulled up at another truckers' picnic spot and soon merrily on their way towards Iraq in yet another truck. This one had a music player and the driver seemed very happy to have company even though only he knew very few words in English.

They went for about an hour along a road with increasingly more pot holes, and as it was beginning to get dark, stopped in a small village. The driver, another Mohammed, said that he would be stopping and pointed into the village, so Keith and Al said their goodbyes and shook hands, put on their rucksacks, with me all the time on Al's head, and walked through the village.

Everybody they passed started waving and shouting greetings with big broad smiles. Not just that though, they started following Keith and Al through the village and out the other side. Few spoke

English. Most of the men wore Arab style dress and most of the children were bare-footed in virtual rags. We passed various shops, stalls and tea-houses – where men were sitting in the street – there was not a woman to be seen. By the time we found a place to try to get another lift there was a party of about thirty, mostly children, behind us and as soon as a vehicle came along and Keith and Al started waving their hands asking for a ride, all the children and adults started doing the same!

Keith said: "Aw man, we'll never get a lift like this – it looks like we're at the end of a long line of people wanting a lift too, man," as he started trying to motion to some of them to move away. But as he waved them away they came closer.

Al laughed and said "I think that wave you're doing means 'come here'! I'll just go and tell them."

Finally Al walked over to one of the adults and asked if anyone spoke English. He discovered by chance that he had chosen the village schoolteacher who did indeed understand. Al explained that we were in a hurry to reach the border and needed everyone to go away so we could try to get a ride.

"No problem," said the schoolteacher as he walked away leaving everybody else standing there. I could sense the frustration in Al and could see it in Keith. I don't think the Ouzo was helping. Keith started walking further out of the village so Al picked up his bag and followed. The crowd, however, didn't.

As darkness fell and Keith and Al had walked onwards, they could see no lights ahead. There was no traffic on the road, there was nobody about. I don't think Keith or Al's mood was very good at that point.

Suddenly there was a car with no lights coming down the road behind them, honking the horn as if in a panic. It pulled up behind Keith and Al and the headlights went on. Two figures got out of the car and started walking towards them.

"Hello, hello, Sir," said a voice, "we have come to take you to next village." It was the village schoolteacher! He explained that the other man was his 'friend with car' and that they would be happy to take us some of the way on our journey.

The next village was about a ten minute slow drive away, carefully avoiding the many pot holes. It looked like it was going to be a long night. "We'll never get there by midnight," said Al.

"No way man. We're fucked", said Keith.

This was to become a pattern for the next few hours. They would arrive at one end of a village and walk through, gathering a crowd of followers along the way. In one place there must have been over one hundred people – cheering!

From that point somebody would turn up to offer a lift – in a whole variety of vehicles most of them new to me.

There were more trucks and another car, but also a horse and cart, a tractor and almost unbelievably, a motorbike with two men already on it. They sat, first the driver, then Al with his rucksack, then the other man and finally Keith with his rucksack hanging on at the back! We weaved in and out between the potholes for about twenty minutes and pulled into another village. The man said "Passport" and pointed further down the road, indicating with his fingers that we had to walk. "Al Bu Kamai," he said.

It was now 10.30, according to Al, so he said "We've got time for a cup of tea and some food?

"There's a place there, look!"

Keith agreed. The duo drank tea and ate some bread and cheese, some sweet cakes and headed back out of town towards 'Passports'.

"I don't like the vibe here, man" said Keith, "that guy didn't seem like he wanted to serve us. Heavy, man. Let's just get across the border before anything bad happens."

"I reckon so," said Al, "I felt a bit paranoid in there, they didn't seem like the other people in the other villages. Maybe it's because they know we're leaving their country. It's not like we're big spenders!"

So they walked about a mile and arrived at the border with its passport and customs control. The border guard spoke English. "We are closed for the night, good evening," he said, "you cannot go now."

Keith and Al showed their passports and explained that they had a visa but it expired at midnight. The guard kept looking at me, I thought I would end up with a new owner tonight. Maybe he would ask for Al's hat before he let them go through!

"No problem," said the guard, "you sleep here outside and in the morning I give you tea and then you go through, walk to Iraqi border."

It was April 13 1972.

At that time Iraq was governed by President Ahmed Hassan and the al-Bakr Ba'ath Party.

"Another walk through no-man's land," said Al. "I wonder how far that's going to be – last one looked like people lived there and they go back and forth freely to markets and things – if they're in no-man's land they may not even have passports.

Al and Myhat in Al Qa im, Iraq

"We'll take some extra water this time, as it's gonna to be hot walking if it's a long way."

Al and Keith took out their sleeping bags and lay down on the wooden balcony outside the custom's post; the guard brought them some strong and sweet coffee. As they relaxed drinking the coffee, all they could hear were crickets and flying bugs.

The bugs were massive. Neither Al nor I had ever seen anything like them before. They flew around madly targeting the bright lights that were on at all four corners of the custom's building, often crashing into a wall or post. Then they fell to the ground, often landing on their backs and then trying to flip themselves over with their wings. Few seemed to manage that.

As the numbers of bugs increased, the noise grew louder and louder and sleep was retreating. The guard came out with a broom and brushed away the bugs – some took off again and presumably ended up crash landing again, because numbers did not decrease. The guard said "Flippers!" and laughed. This carried on throughout the long sleepless night, every time the guard shouting with glee "Flippers."

The next morning Keith and Al rose quite early, left the border post and walked several miles across no-man's land, where they spotted several small houses and people working in the fields. Keith told Al that they were neither Iraqi nor Syrian people and I figured out they must be no-men and no-women if they lived and worked in no-man's land. Or maybe he meant Norman's land – I had met somebody called Norman once but I did not know if this was where he was from or not.

After an hour or so we arrived in Iraq, presented their visas, changed their money again, this time the money was called Dinars, and walked on into a small village.

"I wonder what this place is called," said Al, "the only sign I saw was in Arabic."

As we arrived in the village we were greeted by several smiling young men dressed in what I realised was typical desert costume of djellaba and sandals.

To say that the village was dry would be an under-statement.

It was parched! There was very little vegetation in sight, lots of dust and sand and many of the buildings seemed to be made of dust and sand too. The main road which led eventually to Baghdad went straight through the village and as we arrived along that road, we saw a tea-house. We headed straight for it, accompanied by some of the young men.

The men were all very friendly and smiling and kept offering Keith and Al cigarettes and black tea. They would not take no for an answer. They wanted to talk and talk in English – as they were all studying English at school.

Al asked one of the men what the village was called.

"Al Qa'im," he said proudly.

Al asked whether there was a way to get to Baghdad cheaply. He knew that it was about three hundred and thirty miles from Deir el Zur to Baghdad and they were not half-way yet.

One of the young men, called Mohammed – a very common-place name and not just in this village apparently - said that the bus was in the early morning and had already left that day, but maybe a truck would pass by. "But," he said, "you have to pay driver same as bus fare – we all pay for lifts in Iraq."

He offered to show Keith and Al around the small village before sharing some food. I sensed some reluctance in Al. He said to Keith: "What about our bags, I don't want to be carrying a rucksack round the village. I am a bit worried if we leave the bags here and one gets nicked, what chance would we have of getting it back?"

Mohammed immediately said "No problem my friends, there are no thieves here. In Iraq we cut off a hand of a thief. You can leave bags here, nobody touch."

"I guess so, man", said Keith.

When Al opened his bag and took out his camera, immediately there was a small crowd eager to get their photos taken. Mohammed organised them in one line and led Al over to join them, whilst Keith took the photo. It must have looked odd with about fifteen local lads dressed in djellaba and sandals, some with head-scarves, lined up with Al wearing a donkey jacket and jeans and with me perched on his head! There was a lot of movement until suddenly Mohammed shouted "Cheese". They all shouted "Cheese" and froze perfectly still. Keith took the photo. It would be along time before that film was developed.

Mohammed and a couple of his friends or brothers walked Keith and Al around the village and took them to their little school. There were few people about, those that were had donkeys and one or two carts laden with figs or dates. Some children, some dogs, a few cars – not a woman in sight!

It was not a large village so the tour took just about half an hour and they returned to the tea house where they were immediately served with couscous and spicy beans with vegetables, dried and fresh figs, goats cheese and unleavened bread, yoghurt and black tea, followed by more black tea, coca cola and endless cigarettes.

Mohammed had asked questions about where we were from,

where were we going, why, what we did at home, did we have wives and children and why not? He wanted to know what life in the UK was like and did we have televisions and telephones. "Have you been on aeroplane?" asked Mohammed.

Suddenly Mohammed turned to Al. "Do you like the Zionists?"

I felt some hesitation in Al before he answered. "There's good and bad in everyone," he said. "Very good answer," said Mohammed beaming. "You are right, but here in our village, only good!"

Later in the afternoon, Al asked if there was a small hotel or lodge to stay the night. Mohammed said "You both stay at my father's house. I take you now?" So this time with their bags, the duo followed Mohammed down a few narrow dusty streets, around a few corners, and eventually stopped at a small one-storey house with a few chickens, goats and dogs roaming around outside. Mohammed's father was called Mohammed! Mohammed senior asked many of the questions that Mohammed Junior had asked and Mohammed Junior translated both ways. It wasn't long before more food arrived. Couscous with spicy beans and vegetables, bread, goats cheese and yoghurt, dried figs and this time olives. There was also chicken that Keith tucked into.

As much as Keith and Al ate, more arrived. Nobody else was eating.

Eventually both Keith and Al said they could not eat any more. Then the three others at the table started eating most of what was left. At this, Al said to Mohammed junior "I hope we have not eaten your dinner."

"No, no," said Mohammed, "you eat first and we eat after, that is our tradition for guests. What is left is for women."

That night as the sun set they went to bed. Fine embroidered quilts and cushions were provided.

The toilet was a small shack down near a tiny stream about fifty yards from the house. One had to take a candle and a bottle of water at night. It was a crouch down toilet, a hole in the ground with a run-off to who-knows where and would not cope with toilet

43

paper. The idea was to use one's left hand to wash oneself with water from the bottle, then wash one's hands afterwards, of course. It was a tradition that everyone kept, to wash or do dirty stuff with the left hand but to eat or shake hands with the right hand. To offer the left hand to shake is a powerful insult and to eat with the left hand is considered dirty, almost obscene. That makes having one's right hand cut-off for thieving even worse – there are probably few with only one hand in Iraq.

In the morning after a breakfast of bread, yoghurt and figs, Mohammed junior led us to the place where we could catch a bus to Baghdad. It was to take almost all day and we passed through the desert. We carried several bottles of drinking water each and some bread, goats cheese, figs and olives for lunch.

"Great people there," Al said to Keith, "this is the first time I've ever been across a desert."

"Yes but it's very hot man and not much to see except sand. Fucking hot," said Keith.

He was right; it was hot, and I spent several hours on Al's lap instead of his head.

They reached Baghdad as it was getting dark and soon found a cheap dormitory near the bus station where they could spend the night. It was cheap enough, even for Keith and Al neither of whom had much money left. It was upstairs above a small eating house where we were told we could eat for free.

The dormitory consisted of two rows of about twelve beds and a few tables and chairs. At one end of the room were gathered about eight elderly men.

"They look like Ali Baba and the thieves, " said Al.

"Hey man, I don't think they're thieves," said Keith; "they've all got two hands."

"Maybe they're clever thieves," said Al, "I am going to tie my rucksack to the bed."

Al kept me on his head all night. Sometimes, tossing and turning,

I would slip off, but Al would stir and pull me back on to his head. It seemed like a long night.

When Al finally decided to get out of bed, I sensed his relief, for not only was there no bad incident, no attempt at stealing his rucksack, but when he looked around, I too could see that those men were not the forty thieves after all. It was a small group of smiling men that soon offered Al and Keith some black tea to drink and some bread and cheese to eat for breakfast. There was no conversation between Al and those men, as it seemed they did not understand Al's language – English – and he did not understand theirs – Arabic. Yet somehow I felt a great sense of friendship between them.

After breakfast, Al and Keith decided to go out into Baghdad and do some exploring. They strolled down a dusty road filled with people that mostly ignored them. There were men dressed either Arab-style or Western-style, women in black, some with faces completely covered and just a criss-cross pattern to look through, others showing their eyes, scruffy children, donkeys, cars, buses and trucks.

"Look!"said Al, "There's a sign saying 'Youth Hostel' – shall we take a look?"

It was a short way up a side street, even dustier than the main street, but, surrounded by a wire fence; it looked spacious and clean.

"I'll nip in and see if they've got rooms and how much, " said Keith. "Might be cheap, man".

Within minutes Keith was back out with big grin on his face: "Its' even cheaper than the dorm, "he said, "and a twin room with a toilet and shower and we can use the kitchen and it's clean too and they even sell food and have table tennis and darts and games."

Keith was really excited so Al went in to take a look and sooner said than done they had booked a room for three nights and moved their bags in.

"Let's not hang about", said Al, "It could be a good day, let's go explore!"

Al and Keith started walking up a wide but dusty street. Al felt very hot. The men he saw were dressed in various ways, some in jeans and T-shirts like Al and Keith, others in flowing robes of various colours and some with cloth wrapped around their heads; others wore suits with or without ties. Then there were what Al assumed were the women underneath what looked like heavy black bundles from head to ankle. He thought they must have been very hot and wondered why they dressed like that – was it out of choice or was it forced upon them.

We passed shops and stalls selling food and clothing, bits and pieces, a butcher's shop with meat hanging from hooks, shops selling books, tools, kitchen items – almost everything and there was a barber or two. There were lots of small Tea Houses and small eateries – and plenty of stalls selling tobacco and newspapers.

It wasn't exactly clean, with a lot of litter and animal droppings, and the dust was made worse by many trucks and buses, and as we progressed up the street there was more and more crowds of people and suddenly we found ourselves in a fruit market.

"Wow!", said Al, "Look at that! Fruits – I'm parched, I want some and wow blackcurrant juices!"

Al and Keith spent the next hour or so wandering up and down the first section of this long street market, trying all sorts of fruit juices and then milkshakes: I remember there were so many different tastes – fruits called raspberry, strawberry, apple, pear, orange, mango, melon and a juice made from carrots. Many of the juices were offered with ice and Al was a bit doubtful as he had been told not to drink tap water, but since the locals were drinking the juices with ice, the lads did too.

We also bought some bread, dates, cheese and olives for later, and some soft cakes. As it was now even hotter, we headed back to the hostel.

The following day Al and Keith spent many hours alternating between sitting outside in the sun and laying on their beds inside, drinking copious amounts of black tea, water and cheap soft drinks loaded up with ice.

"Baghdad is a really old city", said Keith.

"Listen to this, man, it's cool stuff" he said, reading from his travel guide book:

"*Baghdad is the largest city in Iraq and the second largest city in Western Asia after Tehran*".

"Tehran, that's where we're going next!" interrupted Al.

Keith read on:

"*Located along the Tigris River, the city was founded in the 8tcentury and became the capital of the Abbasid Caliphate. Throughout the High Middle Ages, Baghdad was considered to be the largest city in the world with an estimated population of one million, two hundred thousand people.* "

"And the Hanging Gardens of Babylon are not far from here," said Al, "maybe we can get a bus and go there."

But I know that trip never happened for one of the other men in the hostel told them it was not worth seeing, just ruins. I also know that Al regretted not going to see it for himself, ever since.

After a few days in Baghdad that both Al and Keith seemed to enjoy, a couple of visits to the market and an afternoon spent in a museum, we planned an early morning bus to the Iraq-Iran border. That had meant a visit to the Embassy to buy a visa and another change of money.

Iraq and Iran were fighting at some sections along their border but we were told by an information officer at the Tourist office that it was OK where we were going. Iran did not want Iraq money so the plan was to change it at the border.

We were heading for Tehran, about five hundred and sixty miles away. The bus took ages and was crammed to capacity with people wearing all sorts of clothing from complete head-to-toe burkas to T-shirt and jeans. There were just another two Europeans on the bus. When we reached the border town it was almost dark, most places were closed and there was nowhere to stay. Al felt very uncomfortable as soon as they alighted from the bus and people scattered – then the streets looked empty and shadowy.

Trying to cope with a strong feeling of impending disaster, Al and Keith entered a saloon-like eating house that had lights on and an open door. Inside sat a small group of elderly men watching football on a tiny black and white TV. Near the counter sat a small group of young men drinking Fanta and smoking cigarettes – the place was indeed smoky and run-down. Although everyone seemed to turn to look at us as we went in, nobody said a word or even made a gesture.

We went up to the counter and the aged man sat behind it seemed to look straight through us.

"Hello, we would like something to eat please, and some tea", said Keith.

Nothing. It was as if he had not spoken.

Al tried gesturing that he wanted to eat and drink.

The man shrugged and pointed towards the door. I felt Al's strong feeling that we needed to leave.

"Maybe they don't like that we are leaving Iraq," said Keith quietly.

"Well Iraq and Iran are at war in the South if you remember – we're lucky they're not shooting at each other here. Let's go", said Al.

So we left the building and turned left heading again towards the border crossing point that was just a few miles away, Al knew from a sign post with Arab writing and the number 2 pointing that way.

About fifteen minutes later they passed another café.

As we approached, a young man in jeans came out and ran

towards us.

"Welcome, welcome, my friends, you are most welcomed here. The border closed now, you go tomorrow."

"Hello," said Al, "is there something to eat here?"

"Yes, yes, please come, we have food and we have room to sleep and for you my friends no money."

So with thoughts on whether he was once again risking his safety Al followed as Keith headed towards the low door and into a shadowy interior.

There was low music playing and what could have been an extended family with young children crawling or running around. They were almost all dressed like westerners - although the women were mostly covered they did show their faces.

Several people at once gestured to empty chairs and Keith and Al sat down. Everyone was looking at them – and smiling. Immediately glasses of black tea were served up, with biscuits.

Al was sat next to a young man on one side and an elderly man on the other. The young man pointed to the older man and said "My fadda!"

Al turned his head and was met with a massive toothless grin and outstretched hand. "Very pleased you are here now", he said, "You are our guests this night."

Whilst they sipped tea Al and the old man chatted and Al leaned that this was indeed a guest house but they had few guests as they were a big family already and because they were Christians many people passed by. But they were also farmers and were able to grow food for the markets and, said the man "God gives what we need."

The man said his name was Abdullah and he had come to Iraq with his father and mother many years ago, from Turkey. Then they took up farming.

Suddenly a steaming hot bowl of soup was put in front of them, with bread, olives, figs, beans and green vegetables.

"Eat, eat, my friends, this is for you", said Abdullah.

As it turned out few of the family spoke English and over the next hour or so many left. Al was keen to avoid talking politics and anyway he did not know the politics of the area. Abdullah was keen to learn about the places Al had been, asking a lot of questions about his home too.

Close to midnight now, Abdullah showed Al and Keith to two straw mattresses at the one end of the room, where they could sleep.

Keith was reading his travel guide. He said: "Listen to this man. There's two types of Islam, I've been reading about the religion." He read quietly:

"Islam is a monotheistic and Abrahamic religion articulated by the Koran, a book considered by its adherents to be the verbatim word of God.

"Muslims believe that God is one and incomparable[and the purpose of existence is to worship God. Muslims also believe that Islam is the complete and universal version of a primordial faith that was revealed before many times throughout the world, including notably through Adam, Noah, Abraham, Moses, and Jesus, whom they consider prophets. They maintain that the previous messages and revelations have been partially misinterpreted or altered over time, but consider the Arabic Koran, to be both the unaltered and the final revelation of God. Religious concepts and practices include the five pillars of Islam, which are basic concepts and obligatory acts of worship, and following Islamic law, which touches on virtually every aspect of life and society, providing guidance on multifarious topics from banking and welfare, to family life and the environment.

"Most Muslims are of two denominations: Sunni 75–90% or Shia 10–20%.

"Muslims believe that the creation of everything in the universe was brought into being by God's sheer command, "'Be' and so it is," and that the purpose of existence is to worship God. He is

viewed as a personal god who responds whenever a person in need or distress calls him.

"Allah is the term with no plural or gender used by Muslims and Arabic-speaking Christians and Jews to reference God.

"Muslims identify the prophets of Islam as those humans chosen by God to be his messengers. According to the Koran, the prophets were instructed by God to bring the "will of God" to the peoples of the nations.

"Muslims believe that prophets are human and not divine, though some are able to perform miracles to prove their claim. Islamic theology says that all of God's messengers preached the message of Islam—submission to the will of God. The Koran mentions the names of numerous figures considered prophets in Islam, including Adam, Noah, Abraham, Moses and Jesus, among others.

"Muslims believe that God finally sent Muhammad as the last prophet -the Seal of the Prophets - to convey the divine message to the whole world.

"Belief in the "Day of Resurrection" is also crucial for Muslims."

"There's loads more!" said Keith, "about family and what they can and cannot do or eat. They are not supposed to eat pigs or shellfish or become intoxicated. And they're all supposed to do prayers and fast and try to get to Mecca on a pilgrimage once in their lives – I think that's in Saudi Arabia."

Next thing I knew it was morning, April 18 1972, and we were sitting outside at a wooden table with Abdullah and a few others, eating yoghurt and bread and figs with cheeses and pickles – and marmalade! Abdullah's son came out with a camera and happy photos were taken – Al never got to see them though.

Al and Keith left and walked for about half an hour to the border where they changed money, went through formalities, and then boarded a bus to Tehran in Iran. The small village where they caught the bus, not far from the border, was the opposite of the town Al had hated the night before.

The street and its buildings were clean and almost modern, people saying hello and smiling,   It looked quite busy with cars and trucks and quite welcoming. Al wondered why it was so close but so different to the other place he realised now that he did not even know the name of the place. He thought for a moment that Abdullah and his house may have been a dream.

But almost a soon as they found the bus station office, it was time to get on the bus to Tehran which would take all day again.

Iran was being ruled by Shah Mohammed Reza Shah Pahlav, basically a king.

This time there were no Europeans but there was a Russian man on the next seat and as soon as he found out that Al and Keith spoke English he started talking loudly to them and did so for most of the day. He had food to share, fruit and bread and cheeses, so everyone was happy.

We arrived in Tehran just as it was getting dark and immediately we spotted a hostel near the main bus station and booked into a dormitory which already housed several Europeans on their way to or from India.

One of them was American John whom they had last seen in Greece before Al and I met – he was the guitar player that they had picked up in their van.

However, the meeting was brief, as both Al and Keith were very tired.

Next morning when Al awoke and put me back on his head, we went outside into a large courtyard and Al joined Keith who was already sat at a table drinking tea and eating bread and fruits. Al sat down and almost immediately a young teenage boy brought him tea, bread, fruit and yoghurt.

As Al was eating, Keith started reading from his guide book again.

"Listen to this, man!" said Keith, "We're in the biggest city in this part of the world.

"Tehran is Iran's largest city and urban area, and the largest city

in Western Asia.

"The city is home to many historic mosques, churches, synagogues."

""There's a lot more stuff here, " said Keith, "more history, culture, climate, religion – but I'm not fucking reading all that out, you can read it later if you want, man."

Al never did read that. Later we went out into the busy street outside the hostel in order to get something to eat. We walked for about half an hour towards the city centre before we found a small eating house. It was a very noisy street and the eatery was just as noisy inside as outside. But inside, everyone seemed to be shouting at everyone else, so Al and Keith decided to sit outside at a wooden table with a plastic table cloth.

There was a menu printed on card but nothing in English, but luckily the waiter spoke English and was able to direct them to some vegetarian food. This consisted of falafels wrapped with flat bread and served with spring onions, bowls of hot and spicy noodles, bean and vegetable stew, a dish of hot broad beans and salads and dips with more bread. They ate their fill. Al felt pleased to get so much food and thought it cheap. Most of the eating places they had passed seemed to be serving mainly meats in bread, or meat in rice. Afterwards they ate a sticky cake with strong black coffee.

"Actually, I wouldn't mind a beer, it's been months!!", said Al.

"Iran is alcohol-free," laughed Keith, "Fuck, you've picked a bad time to want beer man, all these countries are alcohol free and you can get sent to prison for being drunk".

"I guess I'll have to wait 'til we get back to Istanbul then," said Al.

"We'll have to talk about that, man " said Keith, "I know we said we would meet up with Mike and John but that's still weeks away, and I think we should head east across Iran and spend a week or two in Afghanistan it will be a fantastic place with great hash!"

Al and Keith discussed that on their walk back to the hostel. I could tell Al was really keen on getting out of Tehran but at the same time thinking more of an adventure in Afghanistan – which he knew nothing about except they grew cannabis and made strong hash in the mountain areas – and yes they did have enough time.

"I haven't got much money left, " said Al. "I don't want to end up stranded somewhere I don't know anything about – it could be like getting stuck two thousand years ago!"

"Well the best thing is to get some money sent to American Express in Kabul, the capital. If you write a letter now if should be there by the time we get there. It should take a few days.

"We could get a bus to the outskirts tomorrow. We can get a visa in the morning and be hitching a lift by about two o'clock."

So it was decided, that is what they would do, and the next morning we made an early start with out bags and walked into the city – it was more like a Western than Asian city, with streets full of people, cars, trucks and buses. There were no donkey carts and few bicycles. Many of the men were dressed in western styles, either jeans or suits, and the women wore colourful cloths and showed their faces.

Al was surprised that the Embassy was easy to find and the queue to apply for a visa to cross Afghanistan was short. The visa was for up to four weeks. However, they were told that they would have to buy their visas in Mashhad.

They very quickly found a cheap bus to the city outskirts and the road heading East – they would aim for another large town, called Mashhad, much closer to the Afghan border – if they could get a lift. It was six hundred and twenty-five miles by road from Tehran to Mashhad.

Al was wondering what sort of adventure lay in front of them, hitch-hiking with so little money in a country where they knew not one word of the language and was probably going to be very different from Tehran. It was!

As it turned out, a car with two young men wearing jeans and shirts stopped within minutes – and they spoke English. They were not going all the way to Mashhad and said they planned to sleep that night on the edge of the Caspian Sea and carry on next day to their village.

"You can stay few days in our house", said one man, "we have morphine".

"We don't take morphine," said Al.

"Well stay with us anyway," the man said.

Later we learned that these two new hosts-to-be were called Atash and Nouri and were brothers. The car was driven by Atash into the night so by the time they reached the stopping place, it was dark.

By that time Al and Keith had chatted to their new friends and learned that the lads' father was in fact the village and area policeman and that he had a license to grow poppies to make opium. It was opium that the brothers had offered, not morphine itself – morphine was the name they gave to it though. Al asked if opium was legal in Iran.

"Oh no no," said Nouri.

"It is not permitted without special permission to grow and my father has that and anyway he is the police – if you like you can smoke some opium tomorrow – my father will give some for you but only if you want."

"I've smoked opium before, man, it's cool" said Keith; "I really dug it, made me feel relaxed and dreamy. I'd like to smoke some tomorrow. How about you Al?"

I felt that Al was both enthusiastic to try something new and reluctant to take any risk with it. I knew that Al had taken an interest in experimentation whilst at University studying chemistry, after all, that was what science was about and Al was a scientist. Al wondered whether Mike and John whom he had left in Turkey would also try a smoke and thought they probably would – they were chemistry students too.

Al's interest in chemistry had started when he was about thirteen and had been given a "chemistry set" by his father, Jim. From the first time Al had mixed two chemicals (sodium bicarbonate and citric acid) and watched them effervesce, Al's imagination and interest in chemicals had been awakened. Al had thought it was like the two substances had become aware of each other in a "chemical way" and that awareness, he thought, was a form of life.

It was about that age when Al lost interest and belief in any form of god – I knew from his memories that it was due to the behaviour of the minister at the chapel he had been attending for Sunday school – he had seen the way that minister had treated a boy by insulting him and throwing him out because he would not take off his school cap, and Al had not liked it – he felt there was a lack of the love and tolerance that the preacher had talked about. Soon after that Al had opened his eyes in prayers and seen that most of the adults were just standing mouthing the words with their eyes open. When Al looked, there was no light shining, no angels, no god, just people and it had all seemed false and rather funny. So chemistry had come along and Al thought that maybe there was some answers in science as to what the universe was, what life is and why he was here at all.

Those thoughts, not only part of Al's memories but also his behaviour pattern – his need to search and explore, try new experiences and experiment. It was that burning that had taken Al onwards to study chemistry and science at university, but also what had first led him to want to try cannabis – and now he was thinking of trying opium.

Keith, Al knew, was very different in that respect – he had told Al that he did not believe in any gods or any secrets to life and for him, life was just to enjoy – and that was why Keith took drugs. He enjoyed them. That night they slept under the stars by the Caspian Sea. Next morning they awoke early to the sounds of the tinkering bells hanging from the necks of the animals driven by a young goatherd boy. It was a pleasant start to the day. They soon jumped into the car and a few hours later the car pulled into what looked like a large courtyard.

"We eat now", said Nouri, "then we sleep and tomorrow you meet father and maybe smoke – for you my friends, no charge."

The next morning Al awoke to find Keith studying the map in his guide book.

"We can get from here to Mashhad easy I think," he said, "and from there we can get a visa stamp and go to Afghanistan. I'll send a letter home and ask Marion to send us some money to Kabul – maybe you can get some sent out too."

There was a knock on the door and Atash came into the room. "First little food and tea, then to smoke."

"After smoking pipe only little black tea, no food as it will upset stomach and make sick", he said

Breakfast was short and sweet – sweet black tea, eggs and bread and sweet breads, and fruit.

Soon enough Atash led Al and Keith into a large room full of cushions and some of the cushions had men laying on them. Al, Keith and Atash went to one side and sat on some cushions. There was no conversation at all in the room.

In the centre of the room was a man putting a light to the end of what looked like a very long pipe and on the other end was a man laying on his side and sucking on the pipe. Al could see that the man at the lit end seemed to be prodding what looked like a small black ball – and knew that must be the opium.

Atash pointed at the man lighting the opium. "Father", he said. "He speaks no English but good man. He will make pipe for you. Remember, no drinking or eating, only little tea."

It was not long before it was Keith's turn to try the pipe. Keith smoked three pipes as did everyone else in the room and then went back to his cushions.

Then it was Al's turn.

Al noticed how the pipe was smoked through small wooden mouth-pieces and each smoker had their own so that lips did not have to touch the pipe. The room was clean and Al was pleased to see that - and the mouth-pieces – it was nothing like the dark and dirty opium dens Al had read about.

Father, policeman, opium farmer – called Mohammed – took up a small piece of the black opium on a small metal rod which he them placed on the end of the long wooden pipe. Father lit the opium whilst Al sucked gently but consistently until his lungs were full. Mohammed seemed to know exactly how much Al needed, for it ran out of smoke just as Al's lungs were full. Al sucked on three pipes and went back to to relax. The opium had tasted sweet and Al felt a little dreamy.

It carried on like that well into the late afternoon. Al was feeling pretty good, in a dreamy state, not asleep but euphoric. Al did not feel that opium, when used in situations like this, was a bad thing – none of the other smokers seemed anything like the poor decrepit addicts he had read about in the press in his home country. But he was aware that opium was very different to manufactured heroin or morphine. And taking it for a day may be very different to taking it day after day.

Al was feeling very warm and cosy, laying down on the cushions and drifting into pleasant dream-like chains of thoughts. He had smoked about nine pipes!

Mohammed the father had left the room as had most of the other men, when Al opened his eyes and looked around. It was then that he realised that Keith was missing, so he scrambled to his feet and went outside into the courtyard first, to see where his travelling companion was.

To his surprise Al found Keith in a corner by a tree, being sick into a bucket! He asked Keith: "You OK? Doesn't sound too good."

After getting his breath back, Keith stood up: "Aw man, I drank some fucking 7-Up and had some bread and cheeses, it must have been that."

"Well they did tell us not to eat or drink between smoking," laughed Al.

Al at the Opium Farmhouse

"Yeh, that too, man" said Keith.

Al and Keith went indoors and Al took me off his head, a rare occurrence, and I knew nothing until the next morning.

Whilst Al was eating breakfast, he told his hosts that Keith had been sick all night and was still asleep, asking if they could stay another day.

"But," he said, "We won't be smoking today."

"No problem my friend," said Nouri, "We are hoping you will stay and it is our honour to have you and Mr Keith in our house. No smoking, no problem".

It was late afternoon before Keith arose; Al had been spending the afternoon in a shady spot in the courtyard, reading, drinking tea and making notes. He had been looking through Keith's travel guide book, reading a little about Afghanistan, the next country they would visit. They would need to go first to Mashhad and buy a visa, then go by bus to the border. He was thinking just how different everywhere was compared to his home country, Wales, and England where he had been living whilst at University. He was thinking how different University life had been to his younger years at home in his parents' house with his sister and Aunt.

Al's last school as a teenager had been boys only. It had been like that since he was eleven. When he was eighteen, he went to University in a city called Norwich, a day's travel from his parents in Wales. As a University student Al suddenly had complete control over his life, having to pay his rent and buy his food, books and beer out of his money from a government grant. There were also women at the University.

Here in Iran, Al thought, he had hardly ever seen a woman except western or American travellers.

The women there were covered head-to-toe in black clothing. In the village there did not appear to be any at all. It seemed unlikely that many girls or women had much of an academic education. He wondered if there were any at Iranian Universities – were there qualified female doctors or teachers or lawyers? He did not remember seeing any women working in shops or offices, except maybe a few in Tehran. Al thought just how isolated in their lives those women were, probably hardly going outside of their homes or the nearest market. He wondered how much even the men knew about his country and how different it was, especially from this village-come-opium den.

Towards the end of the afternoon, Al spotted Nouri and Atash and asked them if he could take their picture, and they agreed. They stood on a porch outside of a door and put their arms round each other's shoulders and Al took one shot. He had only one film with just about eight shots left.

Nouri asked if he could take one of his brother Atash with Al and it was done.

Now I can tell you that a while later, when the film was developed and printed, to Al's big surprise, whilst his back was to the door and he was facing the camera, a couple of quite young-looking women had opened the doorway, and stood in the background with some small children, one in arms. So there had been women in the village after all? But sadly I was not on Al's head for that photo.

The following day, Atash took Al and Keith by car to a bus stop where they boarded a bus to Mashhad. It seemed like a journey that would never end, a long hot and dusty road in a bus crowded with women dressed in black, men in a variety of garments, and a few live chickens.

Mashhad was well over seven hundred miles from Tehran the way we had travelled – but just one hundred and twenty-five miles from Afghanistan.

Yet we reached Mashhad in the late afternoon, found a small hotel and immediately went out for dinner in a cheap eating house. It was hard to find real vegetarian hot food, so Al resorted to rice with nuts and sultanas called Kabuli rice, and salads. But that was plenty after a hot day on the bus. The next day they would find the Afghan embassy and get their visas.

Keith read a bit about Mashhad out load from his travel guide

"Mashhad is the second most populous city in Iran. It is located in the north east of the country close to the borders of Afghanistan and Turkmenistan. It was a major oasis along the ancient Silk Road connecting with Merv in the East.

"The name Mashhad comes from Arabic, meaning the place of martyrdom the place where Ali ar-Ridha ihe eighth Imam of Shia Muslims, was martyred and so his shrine was placed there.

"At the beginning of the ninth century Mashhad was a small village called Sanabad situated fifteen miles away from Tus. There was a summer palace of 'Hamid ibn Qahtab', the governor of Khorasan.

"Mashhad is also home to one of the oldest libraries of the Middle-East called the Central Library of Astan-e Quds Razavi with a history of over six centuries. The Astan-e Quds Razavi Museum,

which is part of the Astan-e Quds Razavi Complex, is home to over seventy thousand rare manuscripts from various historical eras. There are some six million historical documents in the foundation's central library."

"Maybe tomorrow we can go and see the Imam Raza Shrine – It says it's a Golden Temple," said Keith.

The following morning they arose quite early, as they wanted to see the Temple Shrine and a bit of the city and also had to get their visas. So they headed out, ate a small breakfast at a street café, and started walking, following a small map given to them at the hotel.

The streets were either dusty or muddy. On their journey to Mashhad they had noticed many small settlements or villages that seemed mostly composed of mud huts. But now, despite the mud, the building were of stone. Many were clearly quite old and badly in need of repair.

They found the Embassy first and quickly they had their passports stamped for entry to Afghanistan and permission to stay for up to four weeks – they had to pay for that, but despite shortage of cash it was very cheap, they thought – just "pence".

So after the Embassy they headed to the bus station to find out how much it would cost for a bus the next day – to Herat, a town in Afghanistan about two hundred and thirty miles from Mashhad.

The bus station was awash with mud. They had to literally wade through it, to reach the office, but once inside it was clean and it did not take long to learn that the bus left in the morning and was cheap. First they would have to go to a small border town called Tayebad – in the morning.

By that time the lads were tired of walking and hungry and decided not to visit the Shrine. We went back to the hotel.

The bus journey to Tayebad was incredibly bumpy, often on more of a muddy track than a road, and every time we passed another vehicle there was a great hooting of horns. Definitely not a comfortable ride.

The bus stopped there for an hour or so and then amidst what seemed like total chaos with people loading massive piles of luggage on to the roof, we left for Afghanistan, where the bus would stop for the night in the tiny border village and passengers could find somewhere to sleep, something to eat, and complete the formalities.

Al and Keith were the only Western travellers on that bus – everyone else was from Iran, Afghanistan or Pakistan.

Al and Keith took their rucksacks from the roof of the bus and headed into a wooden shack labelled – in English - "Passport and Customs".

This was close to a small town called Islam Qala.

It was April 24 1972. Inside the shack were wooden tables and chairs and in the corner a window to a small office. At the window stood a line of ten or so people waiting to get their visas stamped. It was all done speedily and efficiently, so there was not too long a wait. Al stepped to the window first, passport in hand, dragging his rucksack. A sad-looking official sat at the window, but as Al approached, he smiled.

"Ah, you from Inglant, why you come to Afghanistan?" said the official.

"Just to see the country and the people," said Al; "We're travelling to India."

"You smoke hasheesh in Inglant?"

"No I don't!". Al thought in this instance it may be best to simply say no.

"Okay, good. You no smoke hasheesh. You no buy hasheesh in Afghanistan. You buy, you smoke, big problem, prison, very bad."

"No, no, we won't smoke it".

With that the official stamped Al's visa and told him he could go through without his bag being searched.

Then it was Keith's turn. Al stood nearby waiting and listening to almost exactly the same conversation again. At the end, Kelth asked if there was somewhere to sleep.

Following the official's suggestion, we left the shack and walked a short distance down a rough road to find a guest house offering "dirt cheap" accommodation, sleeping on rough mats on the floor, in their own sleeping bags. The only facilities were a shared hole-in-the-floor toilet and a shared wash-tap and drain-away sink. But despite his initial impression and appearance, the man on reception smiled and tried to help, although he spoke little English. He was indeed a very large man, at least six foot eight, and wore a long black beard and turban-like hat. He was dressed in a blue suit and white shirt without a tie. He held up a card with the price per person for one night. They handed over some of the Afghan notes that they had bought earlier at the border – the currency was the Afghani. How imaginative, Al had thought.

The room was surprisingly large with space for maybe six people to sleep on the rough dirt floor – which is why it was so dirt cheap, thought Al.

But Al and Keith were the only two to sleep in that room that night.

They sat on the thin mats and were both reading their books, when there was a knock on the door.

Keith jumped up and opened the door to see the reception manager grinning at us.

"You no smoke hash here, big trouble with police!" he said.

"No we are not smoking - we are reading," replied Keith.

"OK said the man, "Do not buy outside."

With that he bowed and walked out of the room, slamming the door behind him.

"Fucking hell, I'm not sure I dig this place," said Keith. "Not sure we'll get a safe smoke if it's all going to fucking be like this."

But within minutes the door opened again and in walked the giant grinning and carrying a large colourful water-pipe hookah. He placed it on the ground and said "I give you some tobacco so you only smoke that, OK. You happy men? Welcome."

Without more ado, he walked out again, this time closing the door more gently.

"What's going on?" said Al. "Seems a weird chap. We said we weren't smoking!"

"Well, we may as well smoke the tobacco," said Keith, "Looks like he may have left something in that newspaper."

Somewhat hestitant was how Al was feeling as he unwrapped the newspaper, wondering in fact what strange thing he was going go find. It was in fact tobacco, chopped up and extremely dry. It was dark brown in colour.

As they had both smoked plenty of cigarettes including the dry rolling tobacco in Turkey, the only new thing here was the hookah itself. It was about three feet high, a round clay bulb and clay neck with a flexible tube to suck on attached, and the smoking bowl at the top of the neck, made again of clay. The whole thing was painted and decorated with short strings of tiny beads of many colours. Al felt it was more of a precious ornament than tobacco pipe.

Keith poured some of the dry tobacco into the pipe, put his mouth to the tubing and a lighted match to the bowl, and sucked – one long, slow but deep suck.

He sat upright holding the smoke in his lungs a while before blowing out a massive cloud of smoke.

He doubled-over, coughing. His colour changed from tanned brown to dark green. He looked like he was about to explode.

But he didn't. A bout of coughing later and he was passing the tubing to Al to try.

I sensed that Al was a lot more wary than Keith had been, as he sucked gently on the pipe. He inhaled and immediately blew out a small cloud of smoke and coughed.

"That's bloody dreadful," shouted Al; "It tastes foul and just made me feel bad, not good. I am not bothering with that."

Just then, once again, the door opened without any knocking, and once again in strode the giant from reception – this time followed by the grinning official from the border control post.

They looked at the hookah and sniffed the air. "Ah, not smoking hasheesh?" said the official with a massive grin.

"Very good.

"Now we smoke good hasheesh. You want to buy, you buy from me OK. It is safe now."

With that he threw his bag to the ground and pulled open the zip. He started to pull out some discus-shaped lumps of black hash.

"I have one hundred grams, or quarter or half-kilo good hasheesh from Mazar. I give you some to smoke, you want, you buy. You not buy, no problem". He bit off a lump of about ten grams from the smaller block and passed it to Al. Al looked at it and then lit a match and warmed the corner of the piece. It smelled fantastic. He passed it to Keith, who took one smell, laughed out loud and proceeded to replace the foul tobacco with some of the crumbled hash.

They smoked a couple of pipes whilst the customs man and reception giant rolled and smoked joints made with American cigarettes.

"You want buy some?"

"No thanks we enjoyed the smoke but we don't want to be taking any with us and don't want to go to prison." said Al.

"No problem, very good very wise," said the official. "In Afghanistan drugs very bad but it is OK here with me but when you go, do not buy drugs."

The official and the giant left the room. Keith and Al moved a cupboard across to place in front of the door.

"Hopefully that'll stop them barging in – I'll roll a joint."

The last cannabis that the lads had smoked was in Turkey, except for the one time with the Americans in the park in Syria, and I can tell you Al was very "high" and enjoying the experience. The two lads spent some time giggling at nothing. They ate bread, cake and fruit that they had bought from a shop on the way to the hotel. Washed down with bottled water.

Al stretched out on the mat, which seemed to be much more comfortable now he was laying down. He fell asleep.

The following morning there was a banging on the door that woke the two travellers, and a shouting from outside:

"Mister come quick, bus to Herat going soon."

So they scrambled to their feet, stuffed their rucksacks, grabbed the remains of their supper, and got out of the hotel, walking fast to the bus stop.

There were a few old cars on the street, and bicycles, as well with the men leading donkeys laden with crops. What was really noticeable was the trucks.

There seemed to be lines of trucks going in each direction, throwing up dust, honking their horns – but it was the way in which the trucks were decorated that was amazing to Al.

Each was painted in bright colours and in unique styles, showing depictions of buildings, people, animals, mountains and lakes. There were trees and flowers, birds and even insects.

Al spotted a truck with an elephant painted on the side, with the trunk going to the cab and then as if raised to the roof. There was one with a lion. There was one with people that looked like men and women dancing together. Several had large birds painted on.

Others were painted brightly in lines and patterns – reds, blues, greens - well almost every colour.

Most of the trucks had a box-like section over the cab, Al thinking that was probably where the driver slept for these would surely involve overnight stops. All the trucks seemed laden to the limit.

Al thought the drivers must be very proud of their trucks – maybe even named them.

When they reached the bus station, it looked like chaos. There seemed to be at least two bus-loads of people with a massive amount of luggage. Huge cloth bundles were being passed up to the roof to be tied down.

Keith walked off and came back a couple of minutes later.

"God man, it's ridiculous," he said, "they reckon that yesterdays bus never left so people had been here all day yesterday waiting, now they want to get on this one.

"Look they're getting bags back down off the roof. The driver said we should get on. I showed him the ticket, he just pointed inside. But I reckon it'll take hours sorting this out. There's still only one bus. Some guy told me this is today's bus and yesterday's bus has broken down so they have to get another one from Herat and that won't be here 'til tonight. Come on let's get on – you get two seats and I'll get the luggage onto the roof. I'll climb up and tie it myself."

So that is what they did – they claimed two seats, put their coats on them. A while later they got off the bus again, for a smoke. Keith had some of his joint from the night before so they went up away from the people to smoke it. It was now about 9 o'clock. The bus should have left at 7.30.

In fact it was almost 11 o'clock before the bus left. The journey was along what seemed like one long straight road through desert, the occasional small village with mountains in the distance.

The bus made several stops at tea houses and once in the middle of nowhere all the men got off for a piss. Keith too. The men lined up and all crouched down, pissing from under their gown-like clothes, mostly grey or white, some with stripes, and a few in blue. Looking out of the bus window, Al laughed. About thirty feet from the road on the sandy ground, in the middle of the long line of crouching men was Keith, standing up with his back to the bus, presumably pissing: dressed in jeans a T-shirt.

It was just then that Al heard an American-sounding voice. "High man!"

Al had not even noticed any non-Asian looking people in the queue or on the bus, but soon learned that sure enough the guy was from the US. He explained that he had arrived from Mashhad three nights ago. He had missed his bus, bought another ticket only to find the next day that bus was broken down. So then this morning he had turned up late, but managed to swap his ticket and paid some money so he could get on this one. From the general conversation, Al gathered that the American was travelling alone and was hating it. Almost everything he said had the word filthy or the words nuisances or stupid in. Al was actually quite glad when the guys started getting back on board and the American went back to his seat.

There was a stop for refreshments, at what was basically a shack with charcoal stoves in the street outside – it was all pretty dirty looking and smoky. People from the bus crowded round barging each other about as if there was a limited supply of gourmet treats.

In fact there was only one choice – a set menu – a watery looking soup and a meat and rice dish, and bread.

Nearby was a tiny stall selling vegetables. Al bought bread and spring onions and a few bottles of Fanta orange drink. That would have to do.

And both vegetable stall and shack café were hassled by flies. Several donkeys in the street, a few dogs, probably open hole-in-the ground latrines. Hardly hygienic. In both the shack and the shop the bread was charred looking, unleavened, covered with flies. The locals did not seem bothered. Al wondered if he should eat anything at all.

The men here were mostly wearing head-coverings that looked

like puffy pancakes, flat hats of grey, white or black wool, called Pakols.

Other men were wearing scarves of varying colours or what looked more like a towel, thrown over their heads.

What women there were wore black garments from head-to-toe and were always seemingly carrying baskets, buckets or bales.

I felt that all the men, seeing me on Al's head, shading his eyes from the glaring sun, wanted me.

Almost all the men wore beards, many quite long. They looked weathered. Al wondered what the American thought of this, but he was still on the bus.

Al was surprised to see the size of all the vegetables and fruit on sale. The spring onions, red and green peppers, tomatoes, apples, melons, onions, carrots were all massive. Two or three times the size he had seen before. There were nuts and open pots of yoghurt sitting in the sun, and bunches of various green leaves. Cans of fizzy drinks and packets of American tobacco were also on sale.

The bus stayed there in the heat for about two hours. Everyone seemed irritated in the heat with nothing to do but wait, but the driver was not going to move. Al fell asleep.

Al was awakened with a bump. The bus was speeding down the new road which was said to have been built across Afghanistan through deserts and paid for with Russian, American and British money. But there was nothing to keep people or animals off the road. Apparently the bus had hit a dog. That was it. The dog was left in the road and the bus carried on.

There were also plenty of Bedouin tents close to the road and sometimes small groups of men leading camels.

Eventually and none too soon, they pulled into Herat just as it was starting to get dark.

It once again looked dusty and ramshackled, the roads far worse than the highway. There were a few cars about, trucks as well as donkeys.

"Hey man, Al, let's get our gear and find a place to stay fast" said Keith, "Before all the rooms get taken."

To Al's amazement their bags were already off the roof of the coach before they got outside, and they immediately spotted a sign across the road that said "Hostel".

They went in; the receptionist spoke English and was pleasant. He said there were many Westerners staying there. He explained that tomorrow many would go on buses to the border or to Kandahar and Kabul. They served an evening meal and breakfast. It was remarkably cheap and looked clean so they booked a room that turned out to have two beds.

The receptionist explained that the bus to Kabul left at 3 o'clock each afternoon and would take almost 24 hours, stopping in Kandahar. He said he could buy their tickets the next morning. Keith and Al gave him the money, about two hundred Afghanis, worth about one pound in British money.

The lads decided to drop their rucksacks into the room, lock the door and go for a walk before it got too dark. The room had two beds with sheets and thick woollen blankets. In the corner was a table and two wooden chairs, and another small table with a wash basin and large jug containing water. They could see the street from the window.

Al told Keith that he had hardly any money left.

That was when Keith first told Al that he had fifty British pounds in travellers cheques that could be cashed at a bank or maybe sold for more on the illicit market – on the street. So really they had no big money problems if Keith would give Al a loan until his money arrived. Al had left Turkey weeks earlier and travelled many miles on less than twenty pounds. Surely they had enough to get to India? Fifty pounds was about two weeks wages in Britain. Al had lived on his "grant" of ten pounds a week for three years, four pounds of which went on rent and the rest of books, bus fares, food and beer. Then he had worked on a building site erecting fences for twenty pounds for five days work. Here in Asia so far, it seemed that twenty pounds was worth more like five hundred pounds.

It was getting dark now and the temperature was dropping quite quickly. They walked up the main street that the bus had stopped on, past tea and coffee houses, small eating places, shops selling foodstuff or with butchers meat hanging as if a feast for the flies, hardware shops with piles of metal and clay cooking pots outside, a baker's shop with a window full of chocolate brownies and other cakes, and shops selling cloths.

They bought some bottles of water, chocolate brownie cakes, rusks, soft cheese, yoghurt and tobacco, and headed back to the hotel.

"Well I can't see there's much here," said Al, when they were back in their room. "What's it say in your book?"

"Aw man I'm hungry, I'll read some later, let's see what they're serving up."

So they went to the dining room in the hostel and to their surprise it was filled with western men and women. Some were sitting at tables eating and others were sat on large bean-bag cushions on the floor. Some of the men had long hair – some short – same for the women. Some were dressed in jeans and T-shirts or sweaters, some in Indian garb – white pyjamas – and a couple in orange robes. There was a girl sitting on a cushion singing and playing her guitar. There were songs by Bob Dylan and Joni Mitchell, as Al recognised.

Al sat at a table and a few of the other diners said "hi".

The man from reception appeared at the table holding a small blackboard with a list of food for sale, in English. Al was amazed to see Pizza, Burgers, Fried Potatoes and Milkshakes listed. But he and Keith decided to try the vegetarian goulash and yellow rice with beans and salad, and a milkshake each.

"Bloody hell, it's cheap," said Keith.

He turned to one of the others and said "Hey man, is the food OK?"

"It's actually very good,"said a chap with an very English accent, "best we've had since Athens." The guy explained that he and his girlfriend were going to Nepal and had left the UK six months earlier. They had chosen to go across Turkey to Iran, rather than the route taken by Al and Keith, but had got stuck in eastern Turkey due to a bad storm and landslide – they had to wait weeks whilst the road was cleared.

They were correct in that, the food was superb and the two ate their fill to the sound of peace songs from the girl on the cushions. Al thought she looked very pretty with her long black hair and smiling face and wondered if she was going to same way as he and Keith.

After dinner and after most of the others had left, Al and Keith went back to their room and Keith rolled a joint with some of the hash he had left. He shared it with Al and then opened his guide book and started to read about Afghanistan.

"It doesn't say much about Herat man," he said, "just that it's a stopping off point for hippies going East or West. But there's a good bit on Afghanistan."

"Do you know, "said Al, "I never heard of it except I remember it from when I collected stamps as a kid, still got some from here. A mystery adventure."

Keith read aloud:

"A landlocked mountainous country with plains in the North and South-West, Afghanistan is variously described as being located within Central Asia or South Asia. The country's highest point is Noshaq, at 24,580 feet - above sea level.

"Despite having numerous rivers and reservoirs, large parts of the country are dry. The endorheic Sistan Basin is one of the driest regions in the world. Aside from the usual rainfall, Afghanistan receives snow during the winter in the Hindu Kush and Pamir Mountains, and the melting snow in the spring season enters the

rivers, lakes, and streams. However, two-thirds of the country's water flows into the neighbouring countries of Iran and Pakistan.

"The north eastern Hindu Kush mountain range, in and around the Badakhshan Province of Afghanistan, is in a geologically active area where earthquakes may occur almost every year. They can be deadly and destructive sometimes, causing landslides in some parts or avalanches during the winter.

"The country's natural resources include: coal, copper, iron ore, lithium, uranium, rare earth elements, chromite, gold, zinc, talc, barites, sulphur, lead, marble, precious and semi-precious stones, natural gas, and petroleum, among other things.

"At over two hundred and fifty thousand square miles, Afghanistan is the world's forty-first largest country, slightly bigger than France and smaller than Burma, about the size of Texas in the United States. It borders Pakistan in the South and East; Iran in the West and China in the Far East.

"Human habitation in Afghanistan dates back to the Middle Paleolithic Era, and the country's strategic location along the Silk Road connected it to the cultures of the Middle East, Central Asia, and South Asia. Through the ages the land has been home to various peoples and witnessed many military campaigns, notably by Alexander the Great, Arab Muslims, Genghis Khan, and in the modern-era by Western powers.

"Excavations of prehistoric sites by Louis Dupree and others suggest that humans were living in what is now Afghanistan at least fifty thousand years ago, and that farming communities in the area were among the earliest in the world. An important site of early historical activities, many believe that Afghanistan compares to Egypt in terms of the historical value of its archaeological sites.

"I'm glad we don't have to remember all that, I always hated having to remember dates in school" said Al.

"Pashto and Dari or Persian are the official languages of Afghanistan; bilingualism is very common. A small percentage of

Afghans are also fluent in Urdu, English, and other languages.

"Over 99% of the Afghan population is Muslim; approximately 80–85% are from the Sunni branch, 15–19% are Shi'a, and roughly 3% are non-denominational Muslims."

"There's a bit about Herat, man, not much though":

"Herat is the capital of Herat province and is situated in the valley of the Hari River, which flows from the mountains of central Afghanistan to the Karakum Desert. The city is linked with Kandahar and Mazar-e-Sharif via highway 1 or the ring road that stretches across the country. It is further linked to the city of Mashhad in Iran through the border town of Islam Qala.

"Situated in a fertile area, Herat dates back to the Avestan times and was traditionally known for its wine."

"Bloody hell, " said Keith, "I didn't think they'd be making wine!"

"Herodotus described Herat as the bread-basket of Central Asia.

"Herat was a great trading centre strategically located on trade routes from Mediterranean Sea to India or to China. The city was noted for its textiles during the Abbasid Caliphate, according to many references in the geographers. The city is described by Estakhri and Ibn Hawqal in the tenth century as a prosperous town surrounded by strong walls with plenty of water sources, extensive suburbs, an inner citadel, a congregational mosque, and four gates, each gate opening to a thriving market place.

"Around three quarters of the population of Herat lives in rural districts while just under a quarter 23% lives in urban areas. Around 50% of the population is male and 50% is female. Dari and Pashtu are spoken by 98% of the population and 97.7% of the villages. Languages spoken by the remaining population are Turkmeni and Uzbeki."

"Hey man I'll read this bit about Kandahar too," said Keith.

"It's the capital of Kandahar Province, located in the south of the country at an altitude of three thousand three hundred above sea level. The Arghandab River runs along the west of the city.

"Kandahar is one of the most culturally significant cities of the Pashtuns and has been their traditional seat of power for more than two hundred years. It is a major trading centre for sheep, wool, cotton, silk, felt, food grains, fresh and dried fruit, and tobacco. The region produces fine fruits, especially pomegranates and grapes, and the city has plants for canning, drying, and packing fruit, and is a major source of marijuana. The area is believed to be the birthplace of cannabis indica."

"Far out, it's where the weed comes from – may get some blindin' stuff there! said Keith."

Keith and Al smoked another joint. Al decided to go to see if they could get a cup of tea, so he left the room and headed to the reception area.

At the reception was the happy friendly man that seemed to be manager, waiter and maybe even cook – and the guitar playing girl from the cushions in the dining room, chatting. From her accent, he guessed she was Canadian.

Al ordered two cups of tea with milk – there was no sugar, just hard boiled sweets to suck on whilst the tea was sipped. Apparently, according to the man, there was often a shortage of sugar but never a shortage of sweets and cakes!

"Hi, I'm Al." He smiled at the girl.

"Hi, I'm Miriam," she said, smiling back. "I'm from Vancouver on my way east." she said.

"I'm going to India," said Al, "At least that's where we're heading now. We left England in a van and we were just going to Turkey and back. There were five of us. But I decided to head east with my mate and the others stayed in Turkey. We're going to meet them later. Well, that was the plan. Now it looks like we're going to India instead."

"So did you come through Turkey and Iran?" asked Miriam.

"Yeah and Iraq and Syria. We were going to go to Beirut but we were put off, so we went to Baghdad instead. We've been on the road a few months now. Actually it's the first time I ever left the UK."

Al felt good chatting to Miriam and they exchanged a few travel tales – talked about the Pudding Shop in Istanbul and how bad it was in Tehran. Al did not mention the opium village though. Miriam did not look the sort that he thought would take opium.

In fact, Al was so busy chatting and sipping his tea that he completely forgot to take a tea for Keith.

Keith suddenly appeared saying "Aw man, where's my fucking tea? I made another number."

He smiled at Miriam and Al introduced them.

"Get some more tea and come and have a smoke," said Keith.

"That would be nice," she said.

So the three went back to the room with tea and smoked a joint, then another. Miriam sat on the bed next to Al. I could tell he liked this girl and wondered what would happen. Would Al leave Keith and go with Miriam? I knew he was thinking of it. Plus it turned out Miriam was catching the same bus to Kandahar the next afternoon.

After an hour or so, Miriam said "Good night, see you!" and left, presumably to her own room.

Now Al was looking forward to the bus journey and maybe chatting with Miriam again and maybe more. With the pleasant feeling from the cannabis and from the girl, he got into bed and soon fell asleep.

Next morning Al was out of bed and quickly down to the dining room for breakfast, hoping to see Miriam there, but she wasn't there.

Breakfast was a big surprise, there was masses. Porridge, eggs, boiled, scrambled, fried, pancakes, sausages and pieces of lamb, which Al did not eat, toast and jams, bowls of massive fruit and even cold pizza, with tea and coffee and fruit juices. After breakfast, Al and Keith went outside to see what the place was like in daylight. Al was secretly hoping he would see Miriam.

The city was dominated by a Fifteenth Century citadel known as Herat Fort. Very impressive but it did not draw Al and Keith to it - neither did they visit the mosque. Instead they amazed themselves simply by walking the street - it was like going back in time a couple of thousand years.

The street was quite busy, with just a few cars and trucks, a lot of donkeys with or without carts, and a camel or two.

Stalls were set up along one side of the road, many offering fruit and vegetables, meat, bread, clothing and kitchen utensils. What traffic there was had to drive past this market on the other side of the road.

There was also quite a large number of elderly men dressed in long robes and turbans, holding out hands or gesturing to eat. Al did not have money to spare for them if he had wanted to give. Many seemed to be given food from the stalls.

Strangely, although it was dusty and hot and looked like something out of Biblical times, obviously not wealthy but mostly unchanged for probably centuries, the place felt really calm and in a way idyllic. Only thing was, no Miriam!

They spotted a sign in English which read "Bus Tikkets Here" (sic). Luckily the man selling the tickets from a small booth spoke English and they were able to make sure that their two tickets would take them all the way to Kabul.

"Yes yes, " said the man, "but you must pay five Afghani extra to reserve seats, five each. You go first Kandahar and then the bus stops for night – you can sleep on bus or get hotel, or stay one day and get another bus to Kabul. But you say now so we keep your seats."

It was two hundred and eighty miles from Herat to Kandahar and another two hundred and ninety to Kabul. Al and Keith quickly agreed that they would stay two nights in the city – the night they arrived and one full day.

"May as well stay, man, if it's where the weed grows," whispered Keith.

So that is what they did. Soon enough they were out of their hostel and it was 3.pm and the bus was leaving on time! Apparently the road to Kandahar, once out of the city of Herat, was in good condition until they entered the city of Kandahar itself.

Miriam was not on the bus and Al felt the journey was disappointing despite the views across the desert to the distant hills and the small groups of Bedouin tents. It went on and on. They arrived in Kandahar when it was dark. The driver pointed them to walk up the street they had just driven down and said "Sleeping there."

Sure enough, there were several hostels and Al and Keith soon found a cheap room with two beds. But there was no food and it was a very different atmosphere to when in Herat. So they dropped their bags and went into a small restaurant near the hotel. It was maybe that they had never heard of vegetarians – Al tried saying "No meat, carne no, nicht Flesh!" wondering if that was Spanish and German at all. The guy with a long black beard, black headdress and grey gown, just shook his head.

Al signalled 'two' and said "Kabul rice no meat' and "two tea." Everyone else seemed to be eating kebabs. Al spotted what looked like omelette; he pointed and said "two".

The food came almost instantly. It was pretty dreadful. The omelette was cold and oily and quite stale; it came with hard crusted bread.The rice was yellow with specks of black and warm rice. Al wondered if it was black rice or burnt bits. He could see there were nuts and raisins in it.

But before Al could even taste the rice, Keith spurted out quite loudly "Man it's fucking horrible, cold and soggy and fuck me look at that – it looks like bits of some animal. It's lamb. You said no meat man, that's no good, I can't eat it."

That put Al off as he pushed the plate of rice aside. He struggled through the omelette.

The waiter brought the tea, black with boiled sweets. He looked at the uneaten food and said something in his language. Keith and Al shrugged and said "I don't understand."

With that the restaurant seemed to come alive. All the other customers seemed to want to take part in a debate. Some quite loud, waving their arms and gesturing at their own plates and at Keith and Al.

"What the fuck's going on now, man,"said Keith, "Sounds like they're gonna lynch us!"

But no, suddenly the place went quiet and one man stood up and said "Excuse me mister, you are speaking English?"

"Yes we speak English," said Al, wondering if it would have been had better if he had just said 'no'.

"Very good Sirs, he say to you ask if food no good. You no want?"

"No we don't like the rice," said Al, "Because it's cold and has meat in it and we said no meat – we don't eat meat."

The man appeared to translate that into a local language and once again the restaurant erupted as everyone wanted their say.

After what seemed to be along debate, the man turned again and said "OK mister no problem, That Kabuli rice with lamb. Only the poor people eat rice with no meat so he think you not have big money and give you meat as gift. No problem mister, you no pay."

"That is very kind but we can pay for the eggs and tea," said Al. "It's because we do not eat animals, no lamb or beef or chickens."

The man translated again and half the restaurant started laughing, smiling and nodding at us. That done, they went back to their hostel wondering if they had made the right decision to stay a day in Kandahar.

That night was quiet; Al wrote letters ready to post the next morning, to some of his friends back in England, asking them to send him some money. Keith had told him to ask people to send it through American Express and to write to "Poste Restante"and the name of any town, and that Al could pick up mail using that at the main post offices. So Al asked for some to be sent to Kabul and some to be sent to Delhi in India.

The next morning they ate bread and curd cheese with fruit for breakfast in a small café next to the bus station, and were soon on the bus on the way to Kabul. They never saw fields of cannabis, as they had hoped for, in Kandahar.

The bus journey was again, unfortunately, not inspiring Al, despite the distant mountains. He was glad when they pulled into the bus station in Kabul, a journey of another two hundred and eighty miles.

Getting out of the bus, Al and Keith were immediately set upon by a group of men offering cheap hotels. Suddenly a man appeared with their rucksacks, asking for money as he had independently climbed to the roof of the bus to get them down. One of the other men said "Take your bags and come, I take you to good cheap hotel Mustafa – do not give money, he not official porter."

So that is what they did.

They walked for about ten minutes and arrived at Hotel Mustafa. It looked clean and was convenient to get to the bus station and the city itself. Inside on reception there were two young men with big gleaming smiles and bright shining eyes beneath their pitch black hair. They were both wearing jeans and shirts.

Al had noticed that there was a greater range of style of clothing – and hats – than elsewhere so far in Afghanistan. Many men wore long coats over trousers. Some even wore suits and shirts but open-necked.

They booked a room with two beds for twenty Afghani per night. Al knew that was very cheap – he had been working forty hours for twenty pounds in England, and twenty Afghanis was worth just a few pence – and that was for two beds.

They paid for seven days in advance. That was almost all of Al's money so he was going to have to depend on Keith.

When he told that to Keith, his friend replied: "No problem man, I have an idea with the traveller's cheques. We should be able to sell them on the street and get more than from the banks.

Inside the room, Keith rolled a joint. There was a small shared balcony but nobody there. So they sat on some chairs at a rickety old table and lit the joint.

Almost immediately one of the guys from reception appeared asking if they wanted tea.

"Yes please," said Al, "With milk."

Minutes later the man appeared again with a large metal pot full of tea, a jug of milk, some sugar and three cups. He pulled up another chair and sat down.

"Where you from my friends?"

"England," said Keith.

"Wales," said Al.

"Welcome to Kabul," he said, "my name is Abdul. My brother is Rafi. We are here for our father's hotel and you are welcome. You want to smoke some good hasheesh. I have chillum."

Al and Keith both knew that a chillum was a clay pipe through which cannabis mixed with tobacco could be smoked and inhaled deeply. They had both, in fact, smoked chillums in England.

So they heartily agreed to share the pipe.

Abdul took a cigarette from his pocket and emptied the tobacco on to his hand. He took a small piece of black hash from his pocket and warmed one end with a lit match before rubbing it into the tobacco and pouring the mix into the chillum. As if by magic,

a young teenage boy appeared with three cups and another pot of tea.

Chillums are usually smoked through clasped hands so that the lips do not touch the mouthpiece. As he waited for his turn, he remembered the occasion of his first smoke. He had been in

Norwich with his friend John, whom he had left along with Mike and the van in Turkey now some weeks ago. Al wondered briefly where John and Mike were. He wondered if there would be news in a letter at the Post Office.

Al was thinking of that one fine day when he and John had been walking into Norwich city centre. They had been smoking some fine Lebanese hash the night before – it was a sort of green brown colour but when rolled between fingers it turned reddish and dark – a good sign.

As they walked close to Chapelfield Gardens, walking towards them was a large clean-cut chap with a smile on his face. Both Al and John wore their hair long, which is probably why they were stopped.

The guy said "Hi, I'm Paul, just moved here from Australia. They call me Australian Paul, but back there they called me English Paul."

Paul had chatted a couple of minutes about who he was and then asked if Al and John wanted to "score some dope."

They said no. Then Paul had reached over and dropped something into Al's coat pocket, saying "Smoke that later." Al had felt it and realised it may have been a small lump of cannabis. He remembered now how he had expected plain-clothes drugs squa to appear and search and arrest him, but nothing like that had happened.

Instead, Australian Paul said "Tell you what man, let's go have a smoke in the park."

So Al and John, with Al wondering what they were about to get involved with, had gone with Paul to the nearby Chapelfield Gardens where they had sat, whilst Paul rolled a joint – they had smoked it, then another.

By then Al had looked at the piece that Australian Paul had put in his pocket and it had looked just like the Lebanese hash they had smoked the previous evening.

Paul had said: "Tell you what man, give me back that piece and we'll smoke it now. I live in Mill Hill Road, maybe you two can pop round this evening about eight o'clock and we'll have a good smoke."

They had smoked a third joint and Paul had left, telling the lads the number of his house.

As it had happened, Paul lived in the very next street to where Al and John had shared a small flat whilst saving up for their trip. One could almost have seen Paul's place from theirs.

So at about 8 PM they had gingerly knocked on the door, been invited in and met Lorraine, Paul's Australian wife.

Tea had been made and then Paul had produced a chillum. He had warmed up some hash and had rubbed it into some tobacco in his hand, poured it into the chillum and had said "Give me a light man."

Paul had held the chillum between his two clasped hands and inhaled through his hands.

"You know how to smoke this?" he had asked.

Neither Al nor John had ever smoked a chillum before, so Paul showed them how, first passing his clasped hands so each lad could suck on a hole he had made with his hands. "Suck deep, man, from your guts, get a good hit."

Almost as soon as Al sucked he had felt a rush to his head – the tobacco had increased the effects of the cannabis and he had become stoned quite quickly.

Then John had sucked on Paul's clasped hands.

Then they drank tea and chatted whilst Paul prepared another chillum.

This time Paul had shown them exactly how he had clasped his hands around the stem of the chillum, so they could smoke it through their own. It was not difficult.

Over what seemed like the next couple of hours they had smoked several more chillums and drank more tea.

At one point Paul had asked Al to make a pot of tea.

The place was a small bedsit and across the room from where they had been sitting, was a stove, sink and shelves.

Al had put the kettle on the stove but the tea caddy was empty. He spotted a packet of tea, put three spoons of it into the tea pot, poured the rest of the packet into the caddy and added the then boiling water to the pot.

Or at least, he had thought that he had.

Al had gone back and sat on the bed. He had been looking across the room and had seen the lid of the tea pot seemingly rising from the pot! He had thought he was hallucinating!

But when he had risen and gone over to the pot, he had discovered he had actually put three spoons of tea into the caddy and emptied the rest into the pot! The tea had swollen up.

Al, John and Paul had rolled around laughing.

After a while, Al had started feeling hungry and as they had been there at least three hours, had suggested to John that they leave and get some chips. John had agreed.

So they left and walked down to the fish and chip shop that was not too far away, discussing the evening and how strange they had found Paul to be.

They had reached the chip shop but it was closed. Al had wondered what the time was. The streets were very quiet for eleven p.m. He spotted a man walking towards them and asked the time – neither Al nor John wore a watch.

"Quarter to three," said the stranger.

It had been quarter to three in the morning – they had been in Paul's place almost six hours!

With that realisation, both Al and John were laughing – in fact they could not stop laughing. They had laughed so much, they had ended up literally rolling round on the pavement clutching their sides!

But after a while the laughter subsided and the two lads went home. That night Al slept "like a log".

Al smoked many chillums after that and that included smoking with Keith as well as Paul and John.

That had been Al's introduction to a chillum and that was how he knew Keith could smoke them too.

Now in Kabul, he was about to smoke a chillum of unknown strength, with Keith and Abdul. He was looking forward to it, and soon enough they were puffing away and feeling very good. Abdul told them that if they wanted more hash, he would buy for them, or they could buy from "boy in street with cigarettes".

Al enjoyed the smoke – he and Keith laughed at nothing once they were back in their room. Al lay on his bed and was soon asleep.

He awoke some hours later. Keith was snoring, but awoke soon after Al started moving. Al went to reception to get some tea and when he returned, Keith was making another chillum.

They smoked the chillum and drank the tea, joked and laughed for a while, then fell asleep again.

When they woke up it was the next morning. They left the hotel and went to a small eating house where they ate fried eggs and bread. Nearby was a small shop selling what seemed like almost everything. They bought bread and cheeses, brownie cakes, dry bread rusks, jam, strawberries and yoghurt out of Keith's money.

I noticed a type of hat I had never seen before. Al knew it was called a Jinnah Cap, made from the fur of a breed of sheep, often from the fur of aborted lamb foetuses. The triangular hat is part of the costume of the native people of Kabul which has been worn by generations dating back in Afghanistan. The hat is peaked, and folds flat when taken off of the wearer's head.

They went back to the hotel, smoked, laughed, slept and woke up a couple of hours later.

Keith read from his travel guide:

"Kabul is the capital and largest city of Afghanistan. Kabul is over three thousand five hundred years old and many empires have controlled the city which is at a strategic location along the trade routes of South and Central Asia.

"In the early Twentieth century King Amanullah Khan rose to power. His reforms included electricity for the city and schooling for girls. He drove a Rolls-Royce, and lived in the famous Darul Aman Palace. In 1919, after the Third Anglo-Afghan War, Amanullah announced Afghanistan's independence from foreign affairs at Eidgah Mosque.

"In the 1960s the first Marks & Spencer store in Central Asia was built in the city. Kabul Zoo was inaugurated in 1967, which was maintained with the help of visiting German zoologists. Many foreigners began flocking to Kabul and the nation's tourism industry was starting to pick up speed. Kabul experimented with liberalization, dropping laws requiring women to wear burkas, restrictions on speech and assembly were loosened which led to student politics in the capital Socialist, Maoist and liberal factions demonstrated daily in Kabul while more traditional Islamic leaders spoke out against the failure to aid the Afghan countryside."

They ate some snacks that they had bought and decided to go out for a walk. Outside the hotel they saw a boy of maybe fourteen years in the street near the hotel. He was selling cigarettes – one could buy a packet or just a few. Keith bought a few and the boy offered a small piece of hash, which Keith also bought. The boy said "Mister, be careful, only buy hasheesh from me – it is very good – others selling bad hasheesh and maybe big problem for you."

Al and Keith went walking down the street and soon reached

the river. Looking back at the town behind them it seemed like a building site – piles of rubble, holes in the road, buildings tumbling down. On the other side of the river there were many houses built on the hill.

The streets this side were busy with people, many carrying baskets and some of them on heads – why put a basket on a head, I thought, when they could have had hats. But the baskets contained their wares. Others were carrying massive bundles on their backs.

As we had strolled down this busy street we also saw men sitting on carpets laid out in the street; presumably selling carpets! Others had piles of fruit for sale. Oranges and melons were everywhere. Some stalls were offering slices of melon, with the vendor constantly fanning off the many flies.

Tiny stalls were selling a range of food cooked on small fires or stoves on the ground. Al had no idea what they were selling, but sitting and cooking on the ground like that did not appeal to his sense of hygiene – the place was also littered with trash and animal droppings.

We spotted a man sitting on a wooden chair in the street; behind him was a man who was cutting his hair – a barber. The cut hair fell to the ground and was blown away by the breeze, Next to them was another man giving his customer a shave with a long cut-throat razor.

There were low, covered stalls with rows of meat hanging from the roof – live chickens for sale outside. Other stalls offered cooked lamb kebabs or pieces of chicken, baked potatoes, eggs, breads. Most of them were busy with customers.

There were small stalls selling flowers, shoe-shiner boys, knife-sharpening and stalls with piles of crates of cheap fizzy drinks

The women were all covered head to toe in their long burkas, as they were called, even their eyes were covered with a cross-lattice. Some wore blue, some wore brown and some wore black. Al assumed they were women. Al saw two women walking together dressed in blue burkas; later he saw another two – or were they the same two? He wondered how they would recognise each other in a crowd.

That was of course the local women - the Western women wore either jeans or knee-length dresses showing their legs.

There was a whole range of styles of clothing that the men wore. Some wore long robes and turbans whilst others wore rough-looking jackets or waistcoats over cotton shirts with dark cotton trousers below. Others wore dark suits, and some even wore jeans similar to Al's. There were more Westerners than Al had seen for months. Al wondered briefly if he would see Miriam, but he didn't.

There was also a variety of hats - flat hats, hats made from scarves of white or grey, as well as many different styles of turban, Almost all the older men sported beards.

Most of the male children seen on the streets were either dressed in rags and bare-footed, or like smaller versions of the men; the girls, however, wore dresses, not burkas.

There were many brightly-coloured trucks, buses, cars, bicycles, heavily laden donkeys and even robed men driving sheep or leading a few camels.. There were low-backed trucks filled to overflowing with men, and many buses seemingly filled to capacity too, sometimes with men hanging on at the doorway.

Men were pushing large laden or empty barrows. It was hot, dusty and, in places, smoky or smelly.

Occasionally we saw a couple of police or military dressed in khaki, just strolling round like everyone else, but with batons. A couple of times they were shouting at someone. There were plenty of men and children whose clothes could only be described as dirty rags.

But the view of the mountain was better. There was what looked like a fort on the top. Beyond the river they could see the beautiful hills. It was a great view and they found a place to sit away from people, and Keith rolled a joint. As they looked down to the brown water of the river, they could see women washing clothing and children playing in it.

Al and Keith spent almost a month in Kabul and smoked a great number of chillums and sat at that spot many times.

Al enjoyed discovering the city. But Keith was paying his way. There were no letters at the post office - the Poste Restante – and no money to collect at the American Express offices.

Keith had mentioned several times that he wanted to sell his cheques on the street but the two of them had to go to the Afghan Government building to apply for visa extensions.

Keith sold some cheques, without problem. They simply went closer to the big hotels and waited for a street money-changer to approach them.

Keith gave Al the equivalent of ten pounds in English money, but Al did not feel that would get him very far on public transport and with hotel bills, albeit that it was all so comparatively cheap here. It certainly would not get him to India.

He had a couple of cotton shirts that he sold to the two brothers at the hotel. And a compass set on a plastic base. Al went out with his compass and, seeing a small shop that seemed to be selling junk and second-hand clothes, he entered. Inside was an old man dressed in a brown gown, sitting behind a counter, Al said hello but it was obvious that this man spoke no English.

Al showed the compass and tried to explain its function. He took out a map of Kabul that he had been given by the hotel, and showed it to the man, pointing to the North on the map and to the compass needle. He thought that the man had no idea at all what this was about, but sensed he was fascinated that the needle always pointed the same way, however the compass was turned – it pointed to the door to his shop!

Al knew the symbols for the numbers by now, and gingerly wrote on the back of the map '2000' and said Afghani. The man immediately went to a drawer and came back and gave Al a few bank notes – it was twelve hundred Afghani. He took it happily, although it was only about six pounds in English money it would last for ages here. He could give Keith some money and still have enough – and strangely enough six pounds was what the compass had cost back in England.

By now Al and Keith had found Chicken Street, a street known to be popular with Western Travellers. There were small hotels and eating houses that sold food such as pizzas and burgers, milkshakes and a range of herb teas. Most of the places played Western music, including from Bob Dylan and The Band to Jimi Hendrix, Janice Joplin, Joni Mitchell who made Al think of Miriam, The Doors, The Animals, The Byrds, The Beach Boys, Jefferson Airplane, Captain Beefheart, Frank Zappa, Cream, The Rolling Stones - all the music Al liked - and of course The Beatles and Elvis Presley.

There were several with cushioned rooms and young people smoking joints. They chatted with many of them – some going East and some going West, and heard many strange tales of their experiences, some good and some bad. They heard of a woman supposedly a psychic, at the Pakistan – India border, who seemed to know who had hash and where they had hid it, as people went from one country to the nother. They heard bad stories of how those caught "smuggling" were treated until they paid hefty fines. But they heard worse about the Afghan – Iran border where anyone caught with a kilo could be taken out and shot on the spot. Al had thought how strange that was if the Afghan Customs Officer was selling it!

They spent many hours sitting in those places. On one occasion they had smoked a chillum and gone out wandering and had found a small restaurant and gone in to eat – they both wanted boiled eggs.

It was an upstairs restaurant, quite a large room filled with wooden tables and metal chairs. They sat near the open window with an excellent view of the street below: there were several stalls selling melons and fruits and vegetables, and a couple opposite with smoke blowing across the street, selling cooked street snacks. The ground in between was rough and unsteady and the whole place was busy with men and women, many carrying bundles or pushing wooden carts with big wheels, several riding or leading donkeys and even one man driving sheep, maybe for slaughter in the deeper parts of this street market. Beyond that corner they could see the main street with its various forms of transport.

A boy who looked about fourteen approached them and spoke. It was apparent he spoke very little English but was asking them what they wanted. "Tea with milk" – that seemed to be understood.

"Two soft boiled eggs and toast," said Keith.

The boy looked dumbfounded.

Al decided to try to communicate through sign-language.

He knew the local word for water was "Pani".

So he made a shape like a saucepan in the air with his hands, pointed into the invisible top and said "Pani."

The boy nodded.

Feeling good about that, Al took out a box of matches from his pocket and made like to strike one and hold it under the imaginary now pot of water.

The boy smiled.

Al made a shape like an egg in the air and pretended to place the imaginary egg into the imaginary pot of imaginary hot water – he signalled with two fingers and pointed to himself and Keith.

Meanwhile Keith had come up with his own idea of how to order eggs.

He was crouched down and started flapping his arms and making a noise like a chicken clucking. He pretended to lay an egg and pick it up, then a second egg. Then he pointed at Al and showed four fingers.

The boy smiled and bowed and walked off.

Keith shouted after him, "And toast!"

A short while later the boy returned. He motioned to Al to follow him.

Well Al already knew that often several eating houses would share a kitchen, and that it could be as much as a hundred yards yards away. So he followed the boy feeling confident he would see eggs and bread in the kitchen. Down the stairs, turning right out of the door, up the market street passed stalls selling cloths, about fifty yards or so. The boy stopped and pointed up a short alley. Al could see that it opened on to some sort of yard, but he felt a little uneasy about this. So he motioned the boy to go first, which he did.

When they came out of the alleyway, Al saw that it was a courtyard with closed wooden doors all around and two sets of wooden steps leading up to a wooden veranda with more closed wooden doors. Al looked at the boy and shrugged.

The boy smiled and pointed at one of the doors up the stairs.

"Strange place to have a kitchen!" said Al; the boy obviously did not understand.

The boy waved Al towards the steps, so he ascended and walked along to the door and knocked. There was no answer. He knocked again, with greater force. Still no answer. The boy was shouting something. When Al looked down he saw the boy that seemed to be motioning Al to go in, so he slowly opened the door. He was expecting to see a number of cooks at hot steaming stoves.

Instead he saw a hole-in-the floor toilet! Al laughed out loud – so much for his eggs in hot water act – so much for Keith's flapping and clucking! So much for boiled eggs on toast.

He resigned himself to going back to the restaurant with nothing. He didn't even feel the need to use the toilet.

But as he and the boy were walking back up the street passed the stalls selling cloth, the boy shouted something at the stall-holder and gestured towards Al. The stall-holder motioned for Al to approach and suddenly produced a telephone, on which he spoke. He handed the phone to Al.

A voice on the other end said "Hello, Kann ich Ihnen helfen, was Sie wollen?"

Al recognised that as German. Something like "Can I help, what do you want?" They had tried to teach him German in school for two years but he had had no interest and failed the exams. But he inevitably knew some words and that included the words for four, eggs, water and bread.

" Er ... vier Eier in Wasser mit Brod, bitte" - meaning 'four eggs in water with bread, please.'

"Yah, gut."

Al handed the phone back to the stall-holder who listened and then told the boy.

The boy laughed and pointed back up the street to the alley where the toilet was again, then at Al.

As they walked back to the restaurant the boy kept laughing - he was making a clucking sound!

As it turned out, after Al had returned to Keith and they had laughed about the adventure, they were pleased to see the boy return with tea along with four eggs and a pile of toast. Albeit the eggs were hard boiled but the lads did not care.

f their time in Kabul they ate meat-free Kabuli rice, pizzas, pastas and the lovely baked and spiced potatoes from the street stalls, and plenty of bread and onions and fruit and yoghurt.

They had been in Kabul for three weeks when they heard about the opium den. One evening they decided to try it. Apparently they did not allow cannabis or tobacco to be smoked inside, just opium pipes.

It was a rather dingy looking place off a small courtyard off a dirty back street. There was a man on the door that simply said "Twenty each" and let Al and Keith inside. It was quite dark but Al could see men sitting or laying round on cushions. In the centre of the room was the pipe-maker, sat on the floor, applying a light to the opium on the end of the long pipe that another man was sucking on. The sickly sweet smell of smoked opium reminded Al of that time in Iran and he thought once again he would enjoy it.

Here, however, there was no friendly feeling. It was just a commodity they had to pay for.

They smoked two pipes each and left. Little did anyone know the consequences that were to come weeks later, but I will reveal that at the right time. For now you can only guess.

Instead, they went to Chicken Street to meet friendlier people and smoke some hash.

Chicken Street consisted of stalls and two story buildings occupied by cheap westernised restaurants and shops selling trinkets, clothing, wall hangings and mats, Afghan coats, breads and pancakes, even antique guns and swords – and hats and head scarves – it was where people went to meet and eat or to buy their souvenirs.

"SIGIS" was a popular eating house that we visited many times. It had a courtyard with a giant chessboard.

Other restaurants we visited and sat about in were the Marco Polo and the Khyber.

At the end of Chicken Street was Flower Street where one could buy flowers, fruit and vegetables.

In the restaurants and so-called hippy bars one could meet people with advice on where to stay and they learned of the Hotel Rainbow in Peshawar, in Pakistan, their next planned stop.

We also learned that the Pakistan – India border was closed due to fighting but there was talk of it re-opening soon.

With all those chillums the days passed quickly and before we knew it Al and Keith had bought tickets for a bus through the Khyber pass into Pakistan and Peshawar. That region of Pakistan was called the North-West Frontier and was populated by tribes very different to most Pakistanis.

It was one hundred and forty miles from Kabul to Peshawar, across the Khyber Pass.

On the bus, Keith read quietly from his guide book:

"Peshawar is the capital of Khyber Pakhtunkhwa, formerly known as the North-West Frontier Province,and the administrative centre and economic hub for the Federally Administered Tribal Areas of Pakistan.

"Peshawar is situated in a large valley near the eastern end of the Khyber Pass, close to the Pakistan-Afghan border. Known as 'City on the Frontier', Peshawar's strategic location on the crossroads of Central Asia and South Asia has made it one of the most culturally vibrant and lively cities in the greater region. Peshawar is irrigated by various canals of the Kabul River, Kunhar River and by its right tributary, the Bara River.

"Being among the most ancient cities of the region between Central, South and West Asia, Peshawar has for centuries been a centre of trade between Afghanistan, South Asia, Central Asia and the Middle East. As an ancient centre of learning, the second century BC. Bakhshali Manuscript used in the Bakhshali approximation was found nearby.

"Over 99% of Peshawar's population is Muslim, mostly Sunnis, with Twelver Shias the significant minority group. Despite the mainly Islamic nature of modern Peshawar, the city was previously home to a diverse range of communities, such as Hindus, Sikhs, Jews, Zoroastrians and members of the Bahá'í Faith. A significant number of Sikhs, in addition to smaller communities of Hindus and Christians, continue to exist in Peshawar"

"That is very interesting, I did not know that history", said a voice with a German accent belonging to a man that sat opposite us.

"My name is Hellmut – you want smoke some joint". He had lit up and was offering them a joint – on the bus!

Well, I could tell Al liked the smell so he quickly accepted it with a "Danke" (thank you in German, Al thought). He took three rapid puffs and passed it to Keith who took three puffs and passed what was left back to Hellmut.

Al was feeling quite self-conscious about smoking on a bus heading to Pakistan. He thought everyone was looking.

He turned round to look back down the bus. Almost every seat had a man leaning out and looking back up the bus at him!

And, Al noticed, they were all grinning and smiling and nodding - as if to say "You are stoned now, as we are stoned too."

Al thought those men probably did not smoke cannabis but it must have been in their blood, handed down over the centuries.

It was as if the bus had started gliding.

He relaxed, chatted with Hellmut a while – Hellmut said he travelled that route every year for ten years. Then as the calming effect of the lovely hash took over, he sat and started to enjoy what was to be an incredible journey through the Khyber Pass.

The over-laden coach trundled on, struggling up hills and rounding bends with sheer drops, then doswn and up aga.in. At the end of most down bits there was a small waterfall

At the end of each up bits there was a beautiful view, often including the same road below them, winding around the boulders in between the fields.

At some places there were what looked like caves in the sides of the hills. We passed small groups of men that seemed to be just sitting and looking; we saw young boys driving herds of sheep or goats or camels and several times we had to stop to let them pass us.

Occasionally we saw groups of women carrying baskets, bundles or clay pots on their heads, trailed by urchin-looking children – the children always waving at the coach.

The women here were dressed very differently and, Al thought, more practically than those in Burkas. These showed their faces beneath head-scarves decorated with beads and chains and quite colourful too. These must be tribal mountain women, Al thought.

The coach was moving quite slowly and Al had a chance to take a couple of photographs through the window, of the valley below. He wished he had more film, but thought he would not be able to afford it.

Hellmut was quite jolly company and did lot of talking – they smoked another couple of joints.

He explained that he travelled this same route for years and the border post guards knew him – he always gave them a little money and they left him alone. He also said that every year he visited Afghanistan and Pakistan, India and Nepal, and arranged for shipments of hash to be sent back to London where his partner lived. He travelled for six months, then went back to London and his partner did the same. They were paying off customs everywhere, including the UK, and they were making a lot of money. But, he said, he preferred to stay in cheap hotels, not the big ones, and then he met people.

So Hellmut too, was heading for the Hotel Rainbow.

"Very very cheap", he said, "But it is OK for a few days, but do not eat their food – it is better to go out to eat in a secret local restaurant that I know, it is good and clean."

Hellmut said that after Peshawar, he was heading to Lahore and then would fly to Amritsar where the "Golden Temple" was and where travellers could sleep and eat for free, courtesy of the Sikhs. The same plan as Al and Keith's – they used to call it the "Hippy Trail."

"Hey listen to this about the Khyber Pass man," said Keith, who read again from his travel guide:

"The Khyber Pass is a mountain pass connecting Afghanistan and Pakistan, and cutting through the north-eastern part of the Spin Ghar mountains. An integral part of the ancient Silk Road, it is one of the oldest known passes in the world. Throughout history it has been an important trade route between Central Asia and South Asia and a strategic military location. The summit of the

pass is three miles inside Pakistan at Landi Kotal, at about three thousand five hundred feet.

"The pass itself is entirely in Pakistan. The nearest major cities on the route that goes over the pass are Jalalabad in Afghanistan and Peshawar in Pakistan, with Torkham as border crossing point.

""For strategic reasons, after the First World War the British built a heavily engineered railway through the Pass. The Khyber Pass Railway from Jamrud, near Peshawar, to the Afghan border near Landi Kotal was opened in 1925.

"At the Pakistani frontier post, travellers were advised not to wander away from the road, as the location is a barely controlled Federally Administered Tribal Area.

"Crossing the Khyber has always been something of an adventure. Even in peacetime, this was a fairly wild region where banditry and tribal warfare were part of local history and almost every adult male went armed.

"The area is inhabited by Pathans or Pushtuns, rather fierce Pushtu-speaking hill tribes."

"Did you know that Khyber Pass is Cockney slang for arse!" said Al.

It was quite a journey until they reached Peshawar, but once there, with Hellmut leading the way, they soon found and booked into the Rainbow Hotel. Reception gladly changed Afghani money into Pakistani Rupees.

The room for Al and Keith was small with two beds, but the view out of the window into the street below was good.

It was May 5 1972.

The street looked like a chaotic mishmash of tumble-down buildings with broken or torn flags hanging everywhere. The road was pot-holed. It was crowded with people. There was a restaurant across the road. Al took a photograph – not many left.

There was no toilet in the room. In fact, there did not seem to be one visible at all. So still with me on his head, he went to the reception to ask.

"On roof," said the small man sitting behind a desk reading a newspaper. He did not seen interested.

Al climbed two flights of stairs to find a door that opened onto the roof.

In the middle of the roof was a wooden structure with three doors, a couple of steps up and inside there was a hole in the concrete floor and a jug of water. The water was to wash instead of the Western toilet papers we had seen in some cities.

Below the hole was another level of concrete – piled with human shit. It was smelling real bad even though the day was cooling fast as the light was beginning to fade. The whole place was, of course, swarming with flies.

Later Al learned that the place was emptied once a day, the shit shovelled into wicker baskets lines with rushes and leaves, to be carried down through the hotel and into the street. Al could not imagine what they did with it after that. Those poor women deserved a reward. But he had nothing spare to offer.

A while after returning to the room, there was a knock on the door. Keith jumped up and opened it and there stood Hellmut, grinning and with a smoking joint in his hand.

"Hello my friends, you want to smoke some hash with me and I buy you dinner?"

So they puffed on the joint, their spirits again lifting. Al had been wondering where he was – absolutely everything was so different to his home city; in fact it was so different to anything else he had seen even in the places we had passed through.

Al was thinking, what is different? Well for starters the smells and the air, the people and their costumes, the language and the script, the food and the drink, the streets and the buildings, the transport, the health care, the hygiene and safety rules and protection, life expectancy and family life, even the ways in which business was conducted – people argued over prices.

And, thought Al, what is the same – well I guess I am, he thought – I guess everyone, well most people, have two arms, two legs and two eyes; we're all breathing; we probably all want the same thing,   We all want to achieve something and to find fulfilment, peace, love, freedom.. We probably all wonder at some time what life is all about – or maybe their religions satisfy all that.

Al began wondering why he was travelling – what was he looking for. Religion and science had failed him, now he was feeling like he was wandering far from home, maybe risking his health and safety, taking risks in a dangerous part of the world and with very little money. "Am I nuts?" he thought.

But so far this adventure had gone well, and in any case there was only one direction to go and that was India. Al thought that it was said people could find answers in India – it was where The Beatles had gone to their Guru called Mahesh Yogi. It was a land of many beliefs, supposedly with enlightened beings willing to impart the truth. Or so he'd read. Probably not like that at all. And, thought Al, I probably don't have enough money to buy enlightenment.

Outside in the damp street, the women were dressed in black Burkas again, or colourful cloth wraps, except the Westerners of course. Some of them were well covered too and many wore head scarves. Almost all the Western men wore blue jeans, some with hats of varying sorts, and one even looking quite like myself.

The local men were of two distinct types. One lot were quite short in height and slight, dressed in what often looked like dirty pyjamas with white caps or wrapped in sheets of cloth. The other lot were massive, thick set giants over 6 feet in height, wearing turban-like headgear and armed with rifles and long swords.

Bicycles, three-wheeler Rickshaws, and beasts of burden, were the main form of transport here.

Al spotted a sign above a doorway. It was a drawing of a set of false teeth.   There were three-wheeled street stalls with massive piles of apples, oranges, lemons and yellow and green melons for sale. Dirty-looking streets stalls offered strange looking food in huge pans cooking over charcoal or wood fires.

"You know, my friends, Peshawar is called the 'City of Thieves' – you can buy guns here – be careful with your bags," said Hellmut.

"Fucking great, man," said Keith.

The street was filthy.

"Two nights here then I am going to Lahore on the train, if you want, my friends, I will tell the manager at the hotel and he will buy us tickets," said Hellmut.

"How much do the tickets cost?" asked Keith.

"No problem my friends I am paying, you are my guests. Now we go to special place to eat and we can smoke hashish. It is called The Secret Restaurant and my friend from Berlin, Karl is running it. And his wife Marianna is from Switzerland. They have good vegetarian food and good music there.

The Secret Restaurant was actually inside a large second floor apartment down a poorly lit back street and on to another main road, this time far busier with trucks, carts, colourful coaches, cars and bicycles – and men with donkeys carrying either them or their wares. The roadway and pavements were equally muddy and dirty and it was quite noisy. Street stalls were still selling fruit and vegetables and bottles of fizzy drinks – a lot of signs for Pepsi. Other stalls were issuing clouds of smoke or steam, offering a whole range of quite unpleasant looking foods. Hygiene was an absentee here.

But the apartment building itself, behind a large wall separating it from the road, and guarded at the entrance by a costumed and armed giant from the hills, was remarkably clean.

The guard greeted Hellmut and let us pass through the arched gateway. Hellmut pressed a buzzer near the doorway and soon a pretty young lady came to let us in. Hellmut greeted Marianna, they hugged like good old friends. She led the way for us up the stairs and into the apartment.

The apartment consisted of at least two bedrooms, kitchen, western toilet with shower and a massive living room with a balcony looking out on to what may have been the back garden or a park. There were several round tables with chairs in the room seating for maybe sixteen people. That still left plenty of room for the many cushions scattered around by the walls. About half a dozen people sat at tables another half a dozen or so on the cushions. A young dark-haired girl was playing a guitar and singing 'The Circle Game', a Joni Mitchell song.

For a second or two Al thought it was Miriam, but no.

Al could see outside through a double glass door was a balcony – he could see people were smoking.

The three of us sat at a table; Al took me off his head and put me next on the table next to the fourth chair which was empty. I felt as if I too was a guest at this meal.

The meal was three courses of vegetarian food – two choices for each course.

Al chose dahl with bread, a Madras vegetable curry with rice, and pancakes with fruit. The dahl was a very hot dish made from lentils and onions and garlic. It was all delicious, to Al's taste. And Keith had finished his plates too. Keith had eaten vegetable samosas – triangle of pastry with spicy potatoes and vegetables inside – pasta with creamy sauce and cheese, and rice pudding for afters.

They each drank a beer. It was the first alcohol Al had drank since the Ouzo in Syria. It was not as strong but still went straight to his head. He felt giggly.

Afterwards they smoked chillums on the balcony, looking down on a garden complete with flowers and a small pool with trickling water.

Al was lost looking down at that pool. Suddenly he began to

wonder where he was.

One minute there's a dirty gloomy fearful city at night, with all the hustle and bustle and smoky fumes. Next, a veggie banquet with beer and chillums and Hendrix playing ' Foxy Lady' on a balcony above a heavenly garden. "Maybe in fact", thought Al, "we're actually all dead! Or just sleeping, dreaming. Or being dreamt?"

Al was thinking of the nature of reality - or was it illusion? Science had told him that everything was made of atoms and molecules, forms of energy, but those very atoms were almost all space, with wisp-like clouds of negative charge called electrons around a positively charged nucleus itself made of tiny particles that were sometimes behaving like particles and sometimes like waves – the wave-particle duality. And in between it all, ninety-nine percent was nothing but space. So we are all mostly space.

Al thought that just as ridiculous to believe as a religion saying we were all made out of and by some supreme creator four thousand years ago in the Garden of Eden.

And where was the Garden of Eden anyway? Certainly not in Peshawar.

With that he realised he was sitting on a balcony, high as a kite, looking at a pool of water. They drank another beer and Hellmut led them back to the hotel, this time taking a slightly different, longer but better lit route. Was that fireworks or gunshots we could hear? Guns!

The next day was spent mostly in the Secret Restaurant, smoking, talking and eating.

The morning after that, they took the train to Lahore – in the direction of India. In comparison to the bus rides, the train journey was boring. It was about three hundred and twenty miles but it took many hours.

When we reached Lahore, Hellmut took a taxi to a hotel he knew and we soon booked in. It was another hotel for mostly western travellers.

It was the Hotel Eden! A small place with about a dozen rooms surrounding a small open garden with small shady trees, potted flowers and a pool in the centre!

Eden! Was this the Garden of Eden that Al had been thinking about at the Secret Restaurant in Peshawar.

The hotel also had a games room and Al looked inside; it had a pool table, table tennis and darts board. He went to their room, small but comfortable, with two beds, dressing table with mirror and another table with one chair. On the way in he spotted a machine offering fizzy drinks and bought two for a few rupee coins. There was a massive and noisy fan on the ceiling.

Inside the room, Keith said: "I'll read you a bit about Lahore," and opened his travel guide.

"Lahore is the capital city of the Pakistani province of Punjab and the second largest metropolitan area in the country.

""Upon the independence of Pakistan. Lahore was made capital of the Punjab province in the new state of Pakistan. Almost immediately, large scale riots broke out among Muslims, Sikhs and Hindus, causing many deaths as well as damage to historic monuments—including the Lahore Fort, Badshahi mosque and colonial buildings. With United Nations assistance, the government was able to rebuild Lahore, and most scars of the communal violence of independence were erased. Less than twenty years later, however, Lahore once again became a battleground in the War of 1965. The battlefield and trenches can still be observed today close to the Wagah border area.

"Lahore has a semi-arid climate.

"The hottest month is June, when average highs routinely exceed 104°.

"That's about right, it's damned hot even now in the evening," said Al.

It was indeed one of the hottest places Al had ever been to. At night the choice was beween sweating it out and tossing and turning, awake beneath the powerful and noisy ceiling fan blowing at the bed sheet. In the day it was difficult to move at all.

Hellmut arrived at their room and they smoked joints.

The following morning, breakfast was provided by the Hotel Eden. There was eggs, cheeses, breads, fruits, yoghurt and tea or coffee with sweet and spicy cakes.

By the time they had finished eating, Al was thinking it was already far too hot to move. We sat in the courtyard under the shade of a tree and Al took me from his head and placed me on a nearby table.

Hellmut appeared again and invited Keith and Al to share a "Bhang".

Al knew that Bhang was a cold drink made from cannabis and spices, ground together with milk, clarified butter called ghee and water.

The Bhang in fact did not taste very good this time, so Al drank his glassful quickly.

About half an hour or so later and Bhang! The drink lived up to its name! They didn't even go outside of the hotel grounds that day. They spent the day reading and chatting and laughing and eating snacks with tea. Apart from the effects of the Bhang, it was over hundred degrees by noon.

At one time Al decided to go to the games room.

When he entered it was quite dark but he could see what looked like a light switch on the wall half way along, so he went to switch it on. Al put his hand to switch on the light and as he touched it there was a loud bang and a flash.

Al seemed to be flying backwards through the air – he had received an electric shock – first time for him and first time for me. Very strange feeling.

As Al went backwards, time seemed to slow down. Al seemed to have plenty of time to think about what had happened, how stupid he had been in the dark, whether he was about to hit his head on anything and how he would cushion his fall and even what would happen and how people would react back in England if this was going to kill him.

As he landed backwards on the floor, he realised he had not hit any tables or anything and thought about how to best protect his head, so he did his best to keep his head forward and try to take the force of the fall on his back and shoulders.

He bent his head forwards – as he hit the ground I flew off his head, unable to protect him – lucky for him his method worked and the back of his head hit the ground quite gently. But he was pretty much shook up.

He returned to the garden and told Keith what had happened.

Keith seemed like he was in a world of his own, very stoned on cannabis – he did not reply, as if he had not even heard Al, who felt lucky to be alive.

"Hey man," Keith suddenly said, "it's almost four thousand miles direct back to London, we must have done six or seven thousand the way we came."

The next day after breakfast in the garden, Hellmut asked Al and Keith if they would like to join him on a flight to India.

"A few days time, " said Hellmut; "They have opened the border with India and there will be flights from here to Amritsar, I will buy you the tickets, I just need your names and passport numbers. If you want we can fly in a few days after I have done business."

So Hellmut went off in a taxi to buy the tickets. Al and Keith decided to go out and look about the city.

It was about as different, as Al thought, from Peshawar as it is different from Norwich – or maybe less different from Norwich.

The streets were now dusty, not wet, but with less litter and animal droppings.

There were far more cars, taxis, trucks and buses as well as bicycle rickshaws, and far fewer animals of burden. Quite a few bicycles too.

Most of the men were dressed either in one-piece djellabah's, loose-fitting cotton in white or grey, or two-piece cotton garments that looked like pyjamas. A few wore suits, some western-style, others high-buttoned jackets over trousers.

The women wore feminised versions of the same, often with lose scarves draped over their heads, some dressed quite colourfully.

Children were dressed pretty much like the adults! Some men wore the Afghan Jinnah Cap made from sheep's wool, with it's peaked shape and favoured by Pakistani politicians. Others wore oval hats that sat in the middle of their heads not covering the eyes at all. Others wore turbans.

Al and Keith saw stalls on both sides of the street, selling just about everything except the guns we had seen in Peshawar. The buildings were three story and had decorative balconies, many with sheets hanging from them.

Most of the signs were in Arabic writing but some were in English, many offering Pepsi or Seven Up drinks.

There were stalls selling 'lassi', a drink made from crushed ice with milk and yoghurt, with sugar or salt to taste, or fruit juices. The ingredients were scooped up from various aluminium bowls; the ice was piled up behind the vendor who sat cross-legged as he worked. He would lean over, grab a lump of ice and smash it between what Al thought looked like rags. But they were thirsty so they bought and drank some out of aluminium mugs.

That evening they met with Hellmut again at the Hotel Eden, smoked some joints and drank some tea. Hellmut had bought the air tickets for the next day.

"Then tonight I invite you to film studio," said Hellmut. "I am giving some money to make a film. We will have dinner there, it is gut. Also you may meet the top singer in Pakistan and a famous actor. We leave in half an hour when the taxi is coming."

It was a modern-looking building with a couple of guards outside and they just waved us in. Inside the big doors, Hellmut told a receptionist who we were and we were shown through some corridors to a large room decorated with glitter and lights, with pictures of people around the walls, presumably film stars and sponsors.

After a while two young men approached us – they were dressed immaculately in suits and ties.

They shook hands with Hellmut who introduced us simply as "Keith and Al". Obviously in such a place, Al had removed me from his head and I had been placed on a table, so nobody mentioned me. I simply watched, listened and learned.

A waiter came and asked us if we wanted to drink; beer was available, so everyone ordered that. It was American beer. The conversation was mainly between Hellmut and the two Lahore lads.

Sure enough he was going to give them hundreds of thousands of rupees to make a film. They were saying that the industry had suffered. They said they had a top actor and one of the best known pop singers. There was some talk about what the film was about – it sounded that it was mostly about a man and a woman that met and wanted to be together but circumstances always interfered.

After about half an hour, several waiters came in carrying plates and trays of food: bowls of dahl, flat bread, a spicy lamb dish and more pieces of lamb and of chicken, a dish made with chick peas and spice, vegetable curries and rice, yoghurt – and fruits. And a massive cherry tart! And creamy rice pudding. There were five of them eating with enough food for twenty.

Whilst they were eating, suddenly a group of about ten people entered and headed towards them. They were all men except the two women they were surrounding. Apparently one of the ladies was the pop singer.

As they approached the others stopped eating and stood up. Al and Keith did the same. One of the Pakistani hosts at our table spoke, introducing only Hellmut. Smiles were exchanged, but no words and as rapidly as they had arrived, the group left.

"So much for pop stars, man, "said Keith quietly.

After the dinner, we headed back out into a wide corridor.

As Al, Keith and Hellmut headed down the corridor, Al noticed something in another wide corridor off to the left.

There was a group of about ten young men that seemed to be surrounding a girl that Al thought was European. Al thought that did not look like a good situation so decided to look closer.

She was certainly not Pakistani. She wore a headscarf. She looked familiar. She looked a bit like Miriam.

Al started to push his way through the small crowd.

It was Miriam!

"Miriam, hi!" he shouted.

"Al!" she answered and stepped towards him and they gave each other a hug.

Al felt good about that hug.

"You OK, what's happening?" asked Al.

Miriam replied: "I'm OK, great, it's just this lot, they think I'm a rock star!"

"Well I guess you are!", said Al, "Shall I get rid of them?"

Al turned to the crowd of youths and said "OK, that's enough, now fuck off!"

And, somewhat to Al's surprise, they did!

Al told Miriam that he had better go the exit to tell his friends what he was doing, so they went down the stairs and back towards the long wide corridor that led to the exit.

Suddenly a group of about twenty men were approaching us, all huddled together but still filling the corridor so all Al and Miriam could do was to stand close to the wall as the large group passed by.

Al could see that in the very middle of the group crammed so much that he had to go with the flow, was Zulfikar Ali Bhutto, the President of Pakistan.. Al had the idea he was not entirely popular with people. "Apparently," Miriam said later, "he is on his way to do a TV broadcast, in English as that was the language shared by most of the people rich enough to have a TV."

Miriam told Al that Bhutto had managed to get the release of thousands of prisoners and some territory from India, after signing an agreement with Indira Ghandi, the Prime Minister of India.

When Al and Miriam reached Keith and Hellmut, Al told them he was going to stay a while and drink some beer with Miriam and he would make his own way back to the hotel later. Hellmut passed Al a small paper bag. "It is blues, speed," he said quietly, "Take a few and they will keep you awake and give good buzz".

Al swallowed three tablets and went back to Miriam. They drank coffee instead of beer and chatted for a while. I learned that Miriam had been invited to the studios for dinner by an American but he had not turned up. He also discovered that Miriam had a ticket for the same flight as he for the next day, and that she too planned to stay at the Golden Temple in Amritsar.

After a while Al started to feel the effects of the pills. He was talking a lot! Miriam did not seem to mind, she seemed like a good listener. But Al felt it was time for him to get back to his hotel. Miriam would get a taxi but it was in the opposite direction to Eden. Al saw her into the taxi and was about to order one for himself when one of the young men that had met Hellmut appeared and he offered Al a lift on the back of his moped.

Quite a ride – the "speed" in the blues had kicked in and they seemed to be speeding ever so fast in and out of the busy traffic along poorly lit roads. I thought that I was going to blow off Al's head several times and land in the road and get crushed by a car.

Gladly I was OK and we soon reached the Hotel Eden, Keith sitting in the garden smoking a joint.

So this "speed" drug seemed to make everything go faster whereas the electric shock in the hotel games room and the backwards fall had seemed to make time go more slowly.

"I didn't expect you back tonight – thought you'd be with Miriam, What happened man?" said Keith.

"No I thought I'd better come back and get ready for tomorrow," said Al, "and anyway I don't like those pills, I wanted a smoke."

Several smokes later, his rucksack mostly packed, Al lay on his bed for hours tossing and turning. He just could not get to sleep. Keith was snoring. Al was thinking about Miriam and the flight to Amritsar.

Al had only been in an aeroplane once – I never.

That had been back in his university days. A chemistry friend called Steve was also training to fly a plane. Steve had already accumulated enough hours in the air to be allowed to take a passenger, and had invited a few people to take a short flight over Norwich where they lived.

A group of students had gone to Norwich Airport and met Steve – he showed them the small two-seater plane. Al had been Steve's first passenger that day.

They took off and flew over the city in a large circular flight path. Fantastic views below, Norwich Cathedral then out over the Norfolk Broads and back towards the city, over the University and back to land at the airport. Al remembered how much he had enjoyed that, just two people with such a great sensation and so steady.

Now he was about to take his first "commercial flight" with paying passengers, not yet knowing how big the plane would be, across the border to India, along with Keith, Hellmut and, he hoped, Miriam.

As it turned out the flight from Lahore to Amritsar was only about half an hour and a stewardess gave everyone a fizzy drink and biscuit. It was a small plane but larger than the one he had been in with Steve of course. Every seat was taken. Al was in an aisle seat so did not even get to look down.

The high point of the flight was that Keith had sat next to Hellmut and Al was sat next to Miriam. She told Al she was going to stay at the Golden Temple a couple of days and then try to get a free lift to Delhi and asked Al if he would accompany her. He said yes straight away.

Customs and immigration formalities both sides of the trip were fast, just a stamp in the passports and they were through to collect their bags and get a taxi to the Golden Temple – all four of them

It was May 28 1972.

At the temple, they were met by a friendly Sikh in a turban, who showed them to the shared room, "Boys and girls separate," he said. "You must smoke only outside the rooms. You are very welcome here and please come to big dining room for food, it is given by us to travellers. Maybe tomorrow if you want, go to see Temple?"

Inside the room were four beds – it did not look like any were being used.

Keith read from his guide book:

"Amritsar is a city in north-western part in India. It is the spiritual centre for the Sikh religion and the administrative headquarters of the Amritsar district in the state of Punjab.

"It is home to the Harmandir Sahib commonly known as the Golden Temple the spiritual and cultural centre for the Sikh religion.

"The main commercial activities include tourism, carpets and fabrics, farm produce, handicrafts, service trades, and light engineering. The city is known for its rich cuisine and culture, and for the tragic incident of Jallianwala Bagh massacre in 1919 under

British Rule.

"Amritsar is one of the largest cities of the Punjab state in India. The city origin lies in the village of Tung, and was named after the lake. It was founded by the Sikh Guru Ram Das in 1574 on land bought by him for seven hundred rupees from the owners of the village of Tung.

"The city lies on the main Grand Trunk Road from Delhi to Amritsar connecting to Lahore in Pakistan. "For transportation within Amritsar city, rickshaws, motorised rickshaws, taxis and buses are easily available. It is better to hire cycle -rickshaw in Amritsar than hiring taxi or motor-rickshaw, as cycle-rickshaw pullers are comparatively sober and honest.

"The Harmandir Sahib also known as Darbar Sahib and is informally referred to as the Golden Temple, is a prominent Sikh Gurdwara located in the city of Amritsar, Punjab, India. It was built by the fourth Sikh guru, Guru Ramdaas Sahib Ji, in the Sixteenth Century. In 1604, Guru Arjun completed the Adi Granth, the holy scripture of Sikhism, and installed it in the Gurudwara.

"There are four doors to get into the Harmandir Sahib, which symbolize the openness of the Sikhs towards all people and religions. The present day Gurdwara was rebuilt in 1764 by Jassa

"The Harimandir Sahib is considered holy by Sikhs. The holiest text of Sikhism, the Guru Granth Sahib, is always present inside the Gurdwara. Its construction was mainly intended to build a place of worship for men and women from all walks of life and all religions to come and worship God equally.

"The Gurdwara is surrounded by a large lake or holy tank, known as the Sarovar, which consists of Amrit , holy water or immortal nectar and is fed by the Ravi River. The four entrances to the Gurdwara, signify the importance of acceptance and openness.

"In keeping with the rule observed at all Sikh Gurdwaras worldwide, the Harmandir Sahib is open to all persons regardless of their religion, colour, creed, or sex. The only restrictions on the Harmandir Sahib's visitors concern their behaviour when entering

and while visiting:

"Maintaining the purity of the sacred space and of one's body while in it.

"Upon entering the premises, removing one's shoes (leaving them off for the duration of one's visit) and washing one's feet in the small pool of water provided;

"Not drinking alcohol, eating meat, or smoking cigarettes or other drugs while in the shrine.

"Dressing appropriately: Wearing a head covering is a sign of respect. The Gurdwara provides head scarves for visitors who have not brought a suitable covering;

"Wearing no shoes .

"How to act:

"If you choose to listen to Gurbani, one must also sit on the ground while in the Darbar Sahib as a sign of deference to both the Guru Granth Sahib and God.

"First-time visitors are advised to begin their visit at the information office and then proceed to the Central Sikh Museum near the main entrance and clock tower.

"The Harimandir Sahib runs one of the largest free kitchens in the world, serving one hundred thousand people on average daily. The meal consists of flat bread called chapati and lentil soup called Dahl."

"I reckon we'll check that out tomorrow, man," said Keith. "We have to work out ways to get to New Delhi - it's nearly three hundred miles – I am thinking about jumping a train."

"Yes, what does it say about Sikhism?" said Al.

Keith read aloud again:

"Sikhism is a monotheistic, pantheistic religion founded during the fifteenth century in the Punjab region of the Indian subcontinent by Guru Nanak and developed through the teachings of ten

successive Sikh Gurus, the eleventh and last Guru being the holy scripture Guru Granth Sahib: a collection of the Sikh Gurus' writings as well as poets of other religions, that was first compiled by the fifth Sikh Guru. It is the fifth-largest organized religion in the world, with approximately thirty million adherents. Punjab, India, is the only state in the world with a majority Sikh population.

"Adherents of Sikhism are known as Sikhs which means students or disciples.

"The central teaching in Sikhism is the belief in the concept of the oneness of God.

"There is one primary source of scripture for the Sikhs: the Guru Granth Sahib. The Guru Granth Sahib may be referred to as the The First Volume—and the two terms are often used synonymously.

"Observant Sikhs adhere to long-standing practices and traditions to strengthen and express their faith. The daily recitation from memory of specific passages from the Guru Granth Sahib, especially the Japu, literally chant, hymns is recommended immediately after rising and bathing. Family customs include both reading passages from the scripture and attending the gurdwara , meaning the doorway to God; sometimes transliterated as gurudwara. There are many gurdwaras prominently constructed and maintained across India, as well as in almost every nation where Sikhs reside. Gurdwaras are open to all, regardless of religion, background, caste, or race.

"Worship in a gurdwara consists chiefly of singing of passages from the scripture. Sikhs will commonly enter the gurdwara, touch the ground in front of the holy scripture with their foreheads. The recitation of the eighteenth century and it is is also customary for attending Sikhs.

"The Sikh faith also participates in the custom of Langaror, the community meal. All gurdwaras are open to anyone of any faith for a free meal. People can enter and eat together and are served by faithful members of the community. This is the main cost associated with gurdwaras and where monetary donations are

primarily spent.

"Guru Nanak's teachings are founded not on a final destination of heaven or hell but on a spiritual union with the Akal which results in salvation or Jivanmukta, the liberation of a devotee in the current life before the liberation in the afterlife.

"Guru Gobind Singh makes it clear that human birth is obtained with great fortune, therefore one needs to be able to make the most of this life."

The following morning, Al decided to visit the Golden Temple. It was already very hot, approaching one hundred degrees Fahrenheit. Keith was not feeling so well so decided to stay in the room and sleep.

As Al approached one of the Temple entrances, he spotted Miriam. They greeted each other with a quick and discreet hug and walked together towards the entrance. It was free to go inside.

They had to take their sandals off and wash their feet in a small pool of water.. Then they had to cover their heads – scarves were provided for free: there had been street hawkers outside trying to sell scarves but Al did not buy – at that stage he did not know that he had to wear a head covering.

Al took me off his head and put me into his shoulder bag. By this time I had built up such a level of telepathic contact with Al that I was still able to see what he saw:

Inside the complex, Al saw an incredible marble and golden building set out in the middle of an artificial lake joined by a walkway to the surrounding wide marble pavement and beyond that, white buildings. There were individual and small groups of Sikhs walking around the complex.

The upper part of this ornate rectangular marble structure was covered in gold.

As soon as Al's feet touched the marble pavement he regretted it. Now over one hundred degrees, the marble was almost unbearably hot. There was little shade, little relief. He headed for the water in the lake, sat on the edge and put his feet into the cooling water – Miriam did the same.

Within minutes they were approached by a Sikh wearing a bright orange djellabah's over white trousers and a orange turban.

"Mister and Madam, I am sorry, but please take feet out of holy water."

Al and Miriam immediately removed their feet from the water, the Sikh said thank you and walked off.

Al said "I thought people bathed in this, I thought it was supposed to purify, like the Ganges."

"Maybe we should just jump in and immerse ourselves," said Miriam.

"Could do," laughed Al, "It's so bloody hot my feet are burning. Oops I forgot, not supposed to swear either!"

The two of them stayed for a couple of hours, just chatting quietly and feeling the good feeling. They went back to their separate rooms.

That evening, Al decided to go to find the room where the food was provided, Keith saying that he would join him later.

The large dining room was packed with hundreds of people. Miriam was in the massive hall and sat with a bearded young man. As Al approached, Miriam motioned to him to go and sit with them – she had kept two places for him and Keith. Everyone was sitting on cushions on the floor with cloths laid out in front. Some people were already eating.

Al said hello – he learned that the man, called Sher, was in fact a Sikh who was living as a student in Germany but his home was in India, in Amritsar. Sher told Al that although here he wore a turban over his long hair, when in Germany he took off the turban and let his hair loose like Al's, saying that he seemed to get better treatment there as a hippy rather than a Sikh.

It wasn't long before food arrived. That evening they ate dahl, rice, chapati and yoghurt with sweet Indian sweets and cool water. All lovely vegetarian food.

Miriam said "I've got us a lift to Delhi if you want to come."

"Yes, I'm into that," said Al.

"Sher's father is a mango merchant and tomorrow he will take us to taste his mangoes and then take us to a man that will get us a lift on a truck through the night."

"That's far out," said Al. "I wonder how long that will take, it's about two hundred and fifty miles, I think. Keith's going to try to sneak on a train without paying but I don't fancy that – was wondering about hitching a lift."

Miriam told Al that after she had left Herat, she went direct to Kabul and stayed there two weeks. She must have been there for a least some of the days that Al and Keith had been. She said she had been to Chicken Street and Sigis and had even played her guitar and sang there. But she had stayed on the outskirts. Then she had met up with some Canadian friends who had been driving overland from Europe in a Land Rover. Miriam had travelled with them across the Khyber Pass and down to Lahore. They were staying in a city close to Lahore, and when the border was open and they completed the formalities and repairs to their vehicle, they would drive through to Delhi and then up to Kathmandu in Nepal. Miriam was to meet them in Delhi and go with them to Nepal.

Al and Miriam left Sher having agreed that his father would meet them in that same place the next afternoon; they strolled around the streets for an hour or so, chatting. Al told Miriam the story of getting the boiled eggs in Kabul and she laughed for a long time.

The following day Al was up early and went for breakfast and bought some bread and fruit and water for the journey. He was now really hoping that there would be some money waiting for him at American Express in Delhi.

Al felt that he had been a burden on Keith, and Keith had not been too happy about it. He didn't want to end up being a burden on Mlrlam. He had thoughts of picking up money and going to Nepal with her.

Mid-afternoon, Al had said cheerio to Keith as Keith headed off towards the railway station. He met up with Miriam near the dining hall and soon Sher appeared with an older man, his father, the mango dealer. They called for a three wheeler motor rickshaw with seats for three and waved goodbye to Sher.

Father took Al and Miriam across town, where they tasted yellow mangoes, then across town again to taste green ones, and then back across town to try red ones. Each time he gave them a few in a bag, so now they had about ten of them. But they were all delicious.

Then he took them to the outskirts of town to what looked like a truckers' stop. He took them to a small building and introduced them to an old man with a long white beard.

It was some sort of religious group – there were many old-looking books and pamphlets, including one in English. Al read it – it was some sort of Ashram, a shelter for practices of Yoga and read that the Universe was made by an all-powerful God called ParaBrahman. He realised that the old man was some sort of priest, teacher or Guru – he was very pleasant, constantly smiling – he had a symbol painted on his forehead.

The old teacher chap told Al and Miriam that he had arranged for them to go to Delhi but the truck was not leaving until midnight. He invited them to dinner and soon another delicious vegetarian meal with Nan bread arrived, followed by the Lassi drink flavoured with mangoes!

It was late into the evening before the truck was ready to leave, and Al did not know or care how long it would take to reach Delhi. He had a bag of food, lots of mangos, enough water for a couple of days, and Miriam to keep him company.

When they reached the truck they discovered it was laden high with large rope-tied bundles – they were shown to climb up and found enough space for them to comfortably sit or lay down, in front of the bundles. They set off into the night.

Of course, there was not a lot to see at night but they did pass some lit areas, maybe small towns or villages. They chatted on, shared some joints using hash that Miriam had, and felt good. When it got too cold, they huddled together under Al's sleeping bag.

But suddenly after a few hours the truck halted abruptly and some of the bundles shifted so there was a danger of them toppling down on top of the duo. The truck carried on and every now and then the bundles shifted again. Their space was restricted and Al began to worry for their safety.

He began to try to bang on the roof of the cab to try to get their driver's attention but to no avail. So he thought to try to climb up so that he could dangle something down in front of the cab window so the driver would stop. He used a dress that Miriam took out of her bag.

After a while the truck stopped. The driver got out and Al motioned to him that the bundles were about to topple down. Climbing up, the driver tried pushing up the bundles with Al's help, but they hardly moved. They tried repositioning the ropes. In the end they had made little progress so the driver jumped down and straight away they were on the move again.

Al was still worried about the bundles but the advantage was that Miriam huddled up closer.

So on they travelled until daylight and on into the day, which got hot very quickly.

They made two stops and the driver bought them Chai (sweet milky spicy tea). Each time they tried tightening the ropes. At the third stop, Miriam bought a hot meal for Al and for the driver. It was now late afternoon.

As they were about to climb up to their space on the back of the truck, the driver handed Al a small black lump of what Al now knew to be opium, motioning for him to eat it. Al broke it into two small pieces and he and Miriam ate one each.

It was a few hours later after the opium had induced a sort of slowed-down dreamy state, that, now dark again, the truck was passing through lit-up areas. They were on the outskirts of Delhi and soon the truck pulled up at a large roundabout that Al later learned was called Connaught Circus. They climbed down and the driver motioned across the busy road and made a gesture meaning sleep.

So Al and Miriam tried to cross the road – the effects of the opium did not help. The traffic seemed to be speeding past – trucks, coaches, three-wheeler motorised rickshaws, cars and even donkey-pulled carts. It was taking ages. The traffic seemed non-stop. There was a great honking of horns.

Well, they did eventually get across the road and headed off in the direction that the truck driver had pointed, soon to find a street with several guest houses on. They chose Mr S C Jain's Guest House and was at 7 Pratrap Singh Building just off Janpath Lane. It had dormitories – some for boys and some for girls, no mixed rooms. The dorms were set around a small courtyard with tables and chairs and a water pump. Inside the dorm that Al was shown to, there were six beds, and it looked like three were taken, so he chose one saying hello to his fellow travellers and sat down. One of the other lads started speaking to Al in English: he was German and told Al that he was on his way back to Germany after travelling around India for six months dressed like a Sadhu, in robes with just a begging bowl and chillum. Al knew that Sadhu's were supposed to relinquish all their possessions and their homes and families, worshipped a god called Shiva and smoked lots of chillums.

Mr Jain said "acha" to almost everything, meaning "OK".

There was a Spanish guy there who spoke English. He told Al about an 'Ashram' called Prem Nagar, in the foothills in the town of Haridwar on the Ganges, the Holy River, where they accommodated people free of charge. Then he told Al about the symptoms of Infectious Hepatitis – a yellowing of the whites of the eyes and the finger nails, how urine would look dark yellow to red, and stools would look pale. Al thought it was strange to be told that.

Then Al went to the courtyard and found Miriam sat drinking fizzy orange. Not having slept a lot the previous night, it wasn't long before Al said goodnight and was asleep.

The following morning when Al awoke, Miriam had already left the hotel but her bags was still there — 'So she would be back!' thought Al. He had a light breakfast from the food and mangos he was still carrying and headed off to find the American Express office to check for money, and then the Post Office to check for mail. He was pleased to find ten pounds waiting from Australian Paul and, at the Post Office, a letter from Paul and his wife.

With that he went back to his dorm and received bad news.

Miriam had made contact with her friends and they were planning to leave Delhi to drive to Nepal the next day. She invited Al to join them.

Al told Miriam that he had so little money and wanted to wait for more, but when he had more he would maybe travel to Kathmandu and leave a message for her at the Poste Restante, hopefully meet up again.

Connaught Circus and the immediate area was quite built-up, with roads off the roundabout in many directions. There was an incredible amount of traffic – it was a busy commercial area and the streets had large buildings, offices, shops and street stalls, some selling strange-looking concoctions of coloured pastes spread onto leaves and sprinkled with Betel nuts – apparently the vile-looking leaves had to be chewed and spat out, and gave an exhilarating effect. Al could see the red stains around the mouths of some of the men – and he could see where it had been spat out on the pavements.

The number of three-wheeler rickshaws was incredible, and any without passengers always seeking work, slowing as they drove past, offering lifts. There were also larger rickshaws carrying eight or more passengers and many over-crowded buses.

Just off the big roundabout was the United Coffee House, in Mohan Singh Place. Nearby was an indoor market where Al found many Sikhs selling their wares, one with cheap triangular vegetable pasties called samosas. Al visited that indoor market many times for samosas or dahl and chapati and fruit-flavoured lassi drink lunches. That was where Al sold his camera, a week or so later.

The walk between Connaught and the hostel was of just about ten minutes but passed an incredibly smelly public toilet to be avoided at all costs. Al learned that water was only available through mains taps for part of the day, so the toilet was seldom cleaned.

This was India and the contrast between rich and poor was striking.

Many of the men wore white Indian Pyjamas, some just rags, whilst others wore western suit and tie. There were many westerners and Japanese-looking people in jeans and shirts, others in Indian-style clothes.

After Miriam had left saying she hoped to see Al again soon, and Keith had not appeared, this was the first time that Al was travelling alone.

He spent about a week in Delhi, checking for mail or money every day, to no avail, but during that week he was out and about every day, visiting New and Old Delhi sights such as the Red Fort and the Jantar Mantar Astronomy Gardens off Connaught Circus.

He learned that the Red Fort, or Lal Qila had been built in about 1648 as a palace by Shahjahanabad, a Moghul emperor, and Moghul emperors had lived there for hundreds of years. It was contained within tall red sandstone walls. The main gate was called the Lahori Gate as it faced the direction of Lahore. Each side of the large gate was a tower. Inside the Fort were rows of buildings and a water channel known as the 'Stream of Paradise'. The Fort was large enough to spend an hour or so wandering around, sitting in the green garden under the shade of trees. It was a pleasant break from the hustle of Delhi's busy streets.After a few days, Al took a train to Agra, to see the Taj Mahal, the world famous white mausoleum built by Mughal emperor Shah Jahan in memory of his third wife in 1632. Mumtaz Mahal, a Persian princess, had died during the birth of their fourteenth child.

Al had arrived at Agra railway station only to find it pouring with rain – the first real rain he had seen since leaving Europe. He took a bicycle rickshaw to the Government's Tourist Bungalow Accommodation and booked a room for three nights – it was very cheap and clean, but the downside was the number of small lizards that were running up the walls and upside-down across the ceiling, and the crickets that seemed to find their way into his rucksack, even his trouser pockets and what is more, inside me, at night. The first morning, Al was constantly surprised when he found them hiding. After that he looked before he put on his trousers and before he put me on his head.

The next morning Al had a quick breakfast of eggs and toast – unlike in Kabul it was easy to order – and took a rickshaw to the Taj Mahal. He picked up a pamphlet from a stall outside that was selling postcards.

"In 1631, Shah Jahan, emperor during the Mughal empire's period of greatest prosperity, was grief-stricken when his third wife, Mumtaz Mahal, a Persian princess, died during the birth of their 14th child, Gauhara Begum. Construction of the Taj Mahal began in 1632.The court chronicles of Shah Jahan's grief illustrate the love story traditionally held as an inspiration for Taj Mahal. The principal mausoleum was completed in 1648 and the surrounding buildings and garden were finished five years later. Emperor Shah Jahan himself described the Taj in these words:

"Should guilty seek asylum here,

"Like one pardoned, he becomes free from sin.

"Should a sinner make his way to this mansion,

"All his past sins are to be washed away.

"The sight of this mansion creates sorrowing sighs;

"And the sun and the moon shed tears from their eyes.

"In this world this edifice has been made;

"To display thereby the creator's glory.

"The tomb is the central focus of the entire complex of the Taj Mahal. This large, white marble structure stands on a square plinth and consists of a symmetrical building with an arch-shaped doorway topped by a large dome and finial.

"Al stood up and absorbed the pleasing view of this incredible white building reflecting in the pool of water that was between the two walkways leading to the marble miracle. On either side there was green grass, bushes, flowers and trees.

There were quite a few tourists about, Indian-looking as well as Japanese and Westerners, and many people taking photographs of their friends in front of the Taj. Al waited for an opportunity and took a photograph. He had just two photos left in his camera and knew that at the moment he did not have enough cash to buy another film.

Al spent about an hour walking round the building and took a look inside – it was all sparklingly clean and well decorated with various types of writing and symbols that we did not understand.

It was a peaceful place to be – unlike many places that we had visited, Al found he could sit without being approached or disturbed by anyone.

When he left, his driver insisted on taking Al to some souvenir shops even though Al stressed he did not want to buy anything. He drank tea provided by merchants whilst they showed their wares. He kept telling them that he did not want to buy, and when he left without buying anything, they did not seem to mind. He saw gem stones, cut and uncut; there were stores crammed with brass ware, from ashtrays of various designs, candle-sticks, goblets and trays and pots small and large. There was a shop selling beautiful marble boxes and table-tops inlaid with slices of semi-precious stones. They also passed many shops selling small models of the Taj Mahal, others seemed to be offering lamps and shades of all types, brightly coloured clothing, beads and jewellery, bags and other leather goods, sacks full of spices and herbs, fruits and vegetables, sweets and breads and several barbers shops – and a stall selling all sorts of hats! We sotted and passed a beer shop.

To Al's surprise he spotted several cows just standing in the streets buzzing with flies, the roadway busy with bicycle-rickshaws and mopeds – Al knew that Hindu's considered the cow to be Holy, did not eat the meat and more or less left the beasts free to roam and munch on whatever they could find to eat.

The next day, Al decided to take a twenty-five mile taxi ride to 'Fatehpur Sikri'.

He read about the place in a book at the Tourist Bungalow and it sounded fascinating. He borrowed the book to take along with him.

"Fatehpur Sikri is a deserted city founded in 1569 by the Mughal emperor Akbar - a planned walled city which took the next fifteen years in planning and construction of a series of royal palaces, harem, courts, a mosque, private quarters and other utility buildings. He named the city, Fatehabad, with Fateh, a word of Arabic origin in Persian, meaning "victorious." it was later called Fatehpur Sikri. It is at Fatehpur Sikri that the legends of Akbar and his famed courtiers, the nine jewels or Navaratnas, were born. Fatehpur Sikri is one of the best preserved collections of Indian Mughal architecture in India.

"The Imperial complex was abandoned in 1585, shortly after its completion, due to paucity of water and its proximity with the Rajputana areas in the North-West, which were increasingly in turmoil. Thus the capital was shifted to Lahore so that Akbar could have a base in the less stable part of the empire, before moving back to Agra in 1598, where he had begun his reign as he shifted his focus to Deccan. In fact, he never returned to the city except for a brief period in 1601.

"Today much of the imperial complex which spread over nearly two mile long and one mile wide area is largely intact and

resembles a ghost town. It is still surrounded by a five mile long wall built during its original construction, on three sides. However apart from the imperial buildings complex few other buildings stand in the area, which is mostly barren."

The walled palace was mostly a pink red sandstone and quite massive. Al had to pay an entrance fee. There were several levels to explore. Al soon found the magnificent Tomb of Salim Chisti, a renowned Sufi saint, with its delicate carvings.

"Buland Darwaza, among the important monuments in the place an enormous gateway has a height of about one hundred and seventy-five feet and is largest gateway in the world. It was made in the year 1575 to celebrate Emperor Akbar's success in conquering Gujarat and is a fine blend of Persian and Mughal architecture."

There were many other buildings to see that he did not read about and also some magnificent views over the walls and across the plain. Al enjoyed the place and vowed to return. He enjoyed the tranquillity, with very few tourists wandering around.

A couple of days later and Al was back in New Delhi by train. He checked the post office – no mail. He checked at American Express – no money.

He decided to sleep in the small local park and save money. The next morning he went again to the Poste Restante. This time there was a letter from a friend back in Norwich promising to send some money in a 'few days.'

So Al decided to best use what money was left and buy a train ticket to Haridwar to try to find that Prem Nagar Ashram that he had been told about, where he could sleep and eat for free, on the Ganges riverbank.

He had now run out of film, so went immediately to the Sikh indoor market and sold his camera.

He bought a big bag of samosas and another bag of fruit, and sooner than imagined was on a packed train to the foothills of the Himalayas. Talk about a crowded train – there were people riding on the roof.

Al had very little idea where he was heading or how long it would take. It took almost twenty-four hours. The train seemed to be taking a zig-zag route, a steam engine pulling us one way then the other, as it travelled up and down the valleys, through places that Al had never heard of. It was supposed to be about one hundred and fifty miles but with all that zig-zag was probably closer to two hundred and fifty.

Haridwar, Al had learned, meant 'Gateway to God' and was one of the Hindu holy places in India and a centre of Hindu religion and mysticism for centuries. It was on the banks of River Ganges and attracted a large number of Hindu pilgrims from all over the world. When the train arrived, it was not long before dark. Al slept that night on a wooden bench at the railway station.

When Al awoke it was really early in the morning. He left the station and found a small café where he ate some breakfast. Whilst he was in there, the waiter recommended that Al go by train to Rishikesh, another of India's sacred Ganges cities. He headed back to the station and yes there was a train in an hour. By now Al had just less than one hundred Rupees and his ticket back to Delhi. He wanted to stay at that ashram for a week and then felt sure that money would be in Delhi when he got back.

All he had was a few dirty rupees notes and a fifty rupees note. The fare to Rishikesh was just five rupees return.

Al queued for over an hour for the ticket which were sold just before the train arrived. When he finally reached the ticket office window and presented his fifty rupees note, he was told that it was no good because it was torn. He was told to go to a bank to change it. Of course that would mean we would miss the train.

So he decided to board the train and he could show the ticket inspector his ticket from Delhi and pay the extra few rupees.

It was not long before the inspector arrived, the train chugging slowly onwards.

Al showed his ticket and explained the problem back in Haridwar.

The ticket inspector said that as Al had no valid ticket, he would have to pay one hundred rupees fine on top of the fare. Of course he didn't have one hundred rupees and said so.

There was a short argument between them and suddenly the inspector turned away and pulled the emergency cord. The train stopped.

The petty official ordered Al to get off the train and, feeling that there was no alternative, he did.

He climbed down, heard the blowing of a whistle and watched as the train pulled away up the track towards Rishikesh. All around seemed like jungle! Al imagined monkeys in the trees and then thought about tigers.

All he could think to do was follow the railway line.

"Bloody petty bureaucrats!" thought Al; "Here I am between two of the most holy cities on the Ganges and I get kicked off a train by an official without compassion."

After enjoying walking for about ten minutes, the track crossed a road. As Al reached the road he spotted a car heading towards the direction of Rishikesh. He waved down the car and it stopped.

Inside the car there was a man and woman and two children, presumably a family, and the man speaking English asked Al if he wanted to go to Rishikesh and offered a lift. The man told Al that he was a Hindu and his name was Ashok. He told Al that he was very happy to meet him and that, if Al wanted, he could spend the day with them. They were planning to visit the ashram of the Maharishi Mahesh Yogi near Rishikesh. Al quickly agreed. Al could hardly believe his luck. Travelling with this family could be far better than on the train.

Ashok told Al a few things about Rishikesh. Al already knew that it was a special holy city on the Ganges, but he was surprised to hear that it is also known as the 'The Gateway to the Garhwal Himalayas'.

Apparently the name means Lord of Senses or Lord Vishnu.

Ashok explained that the Maharishi taught meditation to rich foreigners who paid for their courses. It was called Transcendental Meditation. The ashram was just outside Rishikesh surrounded by trees. Ashok said that normally Westerners were not allowed to look around but Indians could do so, and he thought Al would be allowed inside with them.

"John Lennon and George Harrison and the Beatles and many pop stars from UK and US have come here to learn," he said.

The ashram was within a complex of lecture halls and sparse concrete cells where paying students stayed. The contrast between the luxurious lecture halls and the cells was shocking, as is the contrast between rich and poor throughout India. There were pleasant gardens with many trees where people could stroll or maybe meditate.

It did not appeal to Al at all. He felt he wanted no part of that. How could anyone charge money to supposedly teach peace? After leaving the Maharishi's ashram, Ashok drove first to a small restaurant for a delicious vegetarian lunch. Ashok told Al that Rishikesh was vegetarian by law. That suited Al.

Ashok explained to Al: "Legends say that Lord Rama did penance here for killing Ravana, the demon king of Lanka; and Lakshmana, his younger brother, crossed the river Ganges using a rope bridge."

Now there was a new bridge for locals, tourists, cows and monkeys. Rishikesh was quite full of people in all sorts of styles and colour of clothing – many women dressed in bright coloured sarees. There were also the sadhus and babas that had renounced all worldly goods and wealth and lived besides their holy river Ganges. At this point where two rivers met it was the origin of their holy waters.

The sounds of bells and chimes were everywhere. It was almost like a supermarket for the occult and spiritually-minded, offering courses on well-being and some form of enlightenment, as well as services like palmistry, massages, healing and yoga.

The streets were lined either side with stalls and shops offering, as well as food and drink, amongst other things, gems and semi-precious stones, sarees, all sorts of clothing and shoes and boots, kitchen utensils, wooden goods, books, sweets and cakes. There were street-side barbers, dentists and pharmacies, travel agents and shops offering to tell one's future. The streets were full of the smells of incense and wood fires, mixed sometimes with the smell of cooking or unpleasant drains.

The most astounding sight was the thirteen-storey red temple, called the Tarah Manzil, believed to have been built over five hundred years ago.

The bridge itself, built where Lord Rama's younger brother Laxman was believed to have crossed the Ganges by a rope bridge, was a narrow and swaying suspension bridge. It was used by rickshaws and bicycles as well a pedestrians. At the entrance to the bridge there were monkeys ready to grab what they could from unsuspecting travellers.

The plaque there read:

"Lahshman Jhuala Bridge - first Jeepable suspension bridge of U.P.

"Span - 450 feet; Carriageway - 6 feet.

"This bridge was constructed by U.P.P.W.D during 1927 — 1929. It replaces the old bridge of 284 feet span which was washed away by great floods of October 1924. This was opened to traffic on 11 April 1930".

The views both from and of the bridge with the beautiful mountain backdrops were stunning.

After a pleasant afternoon with Ashok and his family, they drove back to Haridwar and Al was dropped off back near the railway station where, once again, he slept on the wooden bench.

The following morning after a breakfast of fruit, yoghurt and bread, Al took a stroll around the town. It seemed very old. The streets were crowded with people going about their days amidst the cows.

After a while he found a bridge over the river Ganges. It looked greener on the other side, with trees to sit beneath and watch the powerful currents pass. So he crossed the bridge and turned right to follow a rough path running besides the River.

He spotted an orange-robed elderly and bearded man sitting cross-legged beneath a tree, a semi-circle of younger people sitting facing him.

Al knew that they were called Babas, as he himself had been called a few times.

"Maybe he's one of those guru teachers," Al thought.

Back in England Al had read about the pop group The Beatles who had taken up with a Guru called Maharishi Mahesh Yogi who had taught them how to meditate and himself gained great publicity and popularity – maybe it was something to do with that.

The orange-robed 'teacher' shouted something and motioned to Al to go over and join them and sit down. Al complied. The elderly teacher smiled and asked Al where he was from and why he was in Haridwar, in a broken English with an almost German accent.

Al explained that he had travelled overland from the UK, simply on an adventure and that he was here because he had met a Spanish man in Delhi who had recommended it as a good place to stay for a while. The teacher laughed and from under his robes produced a chillum. The chillum was prepared, wrapped in a safi – a small piece of cloth that served as a sort of filter – the tobacco hash mixture poured in and the lit chillum passed around so that everyone including Al had a good puff.

The teacher-come-chillum-maker – the Baba – asked Al if he had a few rupees for another chillum. Al handed over a small note. A young boy suddenly appeared from amongst the nearby thickness of trees, took the note, ran off into the trees to return seconds later with a small lump of black hash which he passed on and which was instantly made into another chillum and smoked.

Al stayed a short while and as nothing was being said and he was quite high on the hash, he said his goodbyes and left, carrying on in the same direction as before. Within minutes he was sitting with another group under another tree, smoking again.

"This is the good life!" thought Al, so high that he was beginning to feel like he was in a Holy city in India. "By the Ganges!"

He left the second group and walked some hundred yards before he had the idea that immersing oneself in the Ganges was supposed to purify the soul.

"Well," he mumbled under his breath so only he (and I) could hear, "Why not, it's hot and I'll soon dry off."

Across the river he could see a long walled building complex with steps going down to the River. As he got closer he could see steps going down on this side too. A few steps, "I should be OK."

The water was moving very fast. Al thought maybe he would not immerse himself, just splash himself all over.

"After all, I can't swim." So he put down his bag, took me off his head and put me on his bag, took off his sandals, and stepped down and into the water.

With some hesitation, one step, second step, third step – then his feet were swept from under him. He felt himself falling backwards into the water which he knew would sweep him away. Too high to feel real fear, he envisioned the situation if he was to be swept down the Ganges – he would have to try to float. He had to hope he would be saved, but who would swim in this? How many bodies had ended up like this. Was this really Holy Water?

As he fell he reached out and somehow managed to grab a chain that was attached to the land, maybe for mooring a boat. He grabbed the chain but the force of the water was now tugging at his body like a hungry monster and now splashing his whole body with his head about to go under.

As his head went under he felt a wrenching on his arm but he pulled stronger, now his head was out, now his body, now he was clambering up the stepsand renched and coughing o up Holy Water. He made it to the rassy bank and collapsed on the ground.

I felt so many emotions and thoughts and images flooding Al's brain.

"So fucking stupid! I could have died."

"Am I cleansed? Am I saved? Don't feel any different."

"God I'm stoned! I shouldn't have done that. What would have happened if that chain wasn't there?"

"Glad I took Myhat off!" So was I.

Had I been in that water I would surely have been swept away for ever.

But it wasn't long before Al was dried out and sitting with yet another group smoking another chillum.

After a while, that particular teacher said that they had seen Al go into the River and now his soul was clean. That was about all he said, except he asked Al if he wanted some chai and said that "Mahatma is coming, he will take you for chai." Al liked the spicy milky tea drinks.

Al wondered if this was the Maharishi Mahesh Yogi or maybe some local lord or lord's son, a rich man probably. Everything was so strange that Al did not know what to expect next. I was wondering about who this 'Mahatma' was - maybe he made hats?

After a while a man in orange robes accompanied by a small group of Indian-looking people approached. Apparently he was the Mahatma. He exchanged words with the teacher under the tree and said to Al: "OK, you come now for chai and this evening we will do our 'Arti' parade through town and then you join us and come to Ashram maybe?" They walked a while, crossed a bridge and entered a small chai shop where the Mahatma said something to the owner or waiter who, seemingly somewhat disgruntled, delivered Al to his table with "No charge, Sir" and the Mahatma and his entourage left, saying "Join us for Arti parade."

There were still a few hours before evening so Al decided to go and wait on his bench back at the railway station.

That was when everything changed.

I sensed that Al's head was spinning, not like it had been after drinking alcohol and nothing like the hash or opium he had smoked or eaten; not even like the blues that he had swallowed in Lahore. This was different, not at all pleasant.

Suddenly Al jumped up and ran to the edge of the platform – he vomited onto the ground. He started to sweat profusely. He felt the need to rush to the toilet which he found just in time and his bowels emptied over the hole in the ground. He was sick again.

A while later he cooled down and felt a little better. He returned to his bench. He was thinking that he had so little money and so few possessions but he had never set out to be a Sadhu, and people called him Baba too!

Now he was ill – he had no idea where Keith was and Miriam was probably in Nepal. He had little or no contact with anyone in the UK. He didn't even really know where Haridwar was. He didn't know where Prem Nagar was. He would have to miss the 'Arti' parade. Was it the holy Ganges water that made him vomit like this – or the reluctantly given Chai?

Now he was sick. He would have to try to get the train back to Delhi and hopefully, some money.

And that is how I, Myhat, felt – like the head, Al, I went with.

And felt I did as felt was part of my fabric.

— The Journey Home —

Whilst Al was on the long journey by train to Delhi and his future, he began to think about what had happened to him on his journey, some of which I never knew.

But first let me remind you a little about myself and then a little about Al and his companions.

My name is Myhat and I am a hat of about sixty years of age.

For some time I had been at a barber's shop in Thessaloniki, Greece: the barber's name was Konstantinos: I had been there for quite a while, often left on a hook, but sometimes when Konstantinos had no hair to cut or chins to shave, he placed me on his head whilst standing in his doorway watching the street.

I was always able to pick up to some extent on what he saw, heard, felt and thought. All I knew of that time was the inside or the shop and the street outside. I understood Greek at that time and just a little English as did the barber.

One fine sunny day my life was about to change, for Konstantinos, spotting a group of young men and a girl walking down the street towards his shop as he stood in the doorway, called and motioned to one of them to come over – and said "Hello, you have no hat. Take Myhat," in English.

He handed me to a young man who put me proudly on his own head. His name was Al.

Al had been a student studying chemistry in a place called Norwich, England, and was now travelling with his companions – John, Keith, Mike and Marion - in a Transit van at that time, to Turkey.

Al had saved up for this holiday for months by working on a building site putting up fences – a big change from his life as a University student at the University of East Anglia studying Chemistry. He had graduated in 1971. John and Mike were also chemistry graduates; Marion had studied biology. Keith, the eldest of the group, had not been at the university and was Marion's partner.

Al thought that Keith was the one with the most travel experiences. Al had never left the UK before.

They had already travelled from the UK, across Belgium,

Germany, Austria, Yugoslavia and then to Greece. The group had had several minor adventures on route, but those stories are for Al to tell at another time. Let it be known that they had all enjoyed their expedition so far.

After I found myself upon Al's head, Al had travelled to Turkey with John, Keith, Mike and Marion, They made their way to southern Turkey and Al had left with Keith to go by boat to the East of Turkey.

From there Al and Keith travelled to India.

Al, Keith and I travelled across Syria, Iraq, Iran, Afghanistan and Pakistan to India.

Al had entered India with a girl called Miriam and spent time with her. But upon reaching Delhi, Miriam had gone with some of her other friends, to Nepal. Al was so desperately short of money that he was unable to go and instead headed for the foothills of the Himalayas where, he had been told, he would find food and bed for free in an Ashram.

So, he had caught the train, visited Haridwar and Rishikesh, smoked many chillums with teachers called Babas that sat under trees and he had immersed himself, almost drowning, in the Hindu Holy River Ganges.

Al's biggest problem had been funds. He had left the UK with just sixty pounds – that was about twelve days work for him. By the time I met him, he had just about thirty pounds.

We had travelled by road in the van, then by boat, cars, trucks, buses, trains, even a tractor and a motorbike – we flew by plane into Amritsar from Lahore.

Along the way they have slept in cheap hotels and camped – all on very little money.

Al smoked tobacco and drank alcohol occasionally, he had also smoked cannabis and on a couple of occasions, opium. We met many types of people and had many experiences that Al mostly enjoyed.

It was the "Hippy Trail" and it was 1972. Al was twenty-two years old, I was about the same age as far as I know.

Throughout the journey I practised what Konstantinos the Barber had often said to his customers back in his shop in Greece – I watched, I listened and I learned.

That was how I was able to inspire Al to write my story, now forty-two years later.

My story restarts with a long and uncomfortable train ride back to New Delhi. We had just left Haridwar, North India. On the railway station Al was vomiting and had diarrhoea. He had very little money, no companionship, wondering where he really was and would he get home.

When we reached Delhi, Al went and stayed in the same small guest house, Mr Jain's, at 7 Pratrap Singh Building near Janpath Lane, that he had used before. Al remembered how Mr Jain used to say !Acha", which means OK, to almost everything.

Every time Al ate or drank anything, he was sick.

He began noticing that his urine was a dark yellow colour and his stools were white. Al thought these were the symptoms of Infectious Hepatitis, so the first thing the next day was to go to a local clinic not far from where he stayed.

When he explained to them his problem, they sent him straight to a Delhi hospital. We were to spend two weeks there, thankfully free of charge, giving Al plenty of good vegetarian food – boiled vegetables, chapati, dahl and yoghurt, so he stopped being sick and began to build up some strength.

The hospital was clean and the staff friendly – a male ward orderly that delivered meals befriended Al and always gave him extra to eat.

Whilst there Al met an aged Indian Hindu man who said that he was dying. But the man had a deep calmness and joy about him – something Al remembers to this day.

On our travels, Al had come across several people that seemed to have that joy about them – he knew not how or why – an elderly Sikh teacher, a Spanish hippy, a Hindu priest, a "Mahatma" in Haridwar on the banks of the Ganges, and now the old chap in the hospital.

He was thinking that maybe there was some sort of answer – one that neither religion nor science had provided him – some sort of key to the meaning of life that would bring peace and joy such as those men had emanated.

Also during his time there, Al had received a visit from a pleasant lady from his embassy who gave him ten pounds. So when he was released, at least he had some rupees.

Two weeks later, after being released from hospital and arriving back in the city, Al went back to his dormitory room and booked in for a couple of nights. Then he went to the American Express offices, as he had written to friends asking for money to be sent there. There was two lots of twenty pounds and one of ten pounds from his friends, waiting for him - a massive boost.

He now had fifty pounds at his disposal, enough to pay his bills and maybe even get back to England – after all he had initially left his home with little more than that, and everything was comparatively cheaper in Asia than Europe.

But, determined to save money, he slept for some nights in a small park close to Mr Jain's Guest House near Janpath Lane, and went each lunchtime to the United Coffee House near Connaught Circus, where, he had been told – and it had proved to be true – rich Indian businessmen went for lunch and would buy Al food simply to be able to practice their English. That worked!

When he had left the hospital, the doctor had told him that no way was he to drink alcohol, and should avoid fried, oily or heavily spiced foods.

Al had discovered a cheap Chinese restaurant near Connaught Circus, where he could eat simple boiled rice with boiled vegetables, so he frequented that.

Early one evening, whilst he was sitting on wall smoking before his meal, he was approached by a pretty young girl – she announced herself as "Diane, from Cambridge" and told us that she had no money and was hungry – she had been abandoned in India by her English boyfriend.

"Can you help me please? I don't have any money." Diane, said.

Al said to her "I won't give you money but I am going over there to that Chinese restaurant and I can never finish my plate of food – so you are welcome to come with me and share – just rice and boiled vegetables though."

Diane immediately said yes and that was the start of another relationship.

That night they huddled together under Al's unzipped sleeping bag in the park and at that time Al told Diane that he had been ill with Infectious Hepatitis so they had better not get too close in case he infected her. He told her about some of his adventures so and that he had just got a little money, so if she wanted, she could travel with him – he planned to leave in a couple of days, by train to Amritsar.

Diane said that she had already phoned her parents in England and they were going to send her some money to Islamabad in Pakistan.

Al had a new travelling companion, some money and was feeling a lot better – maybe the Infectious Hepatitis had gone; certainly the vomiting and running to the toilet had stopped.

The following evening they moved into a room in a cheap guest house called Mrs Colaca's and the following day, Al and Diane went to the Poste Restante to check for mail.

There was a letter from Keith saying that he had been kicked off the train that he had 'jumped' (he had no ticket) but had reached Delhi after a few days. He wrote that he had stayed in Old Delhi but had not seen Al so he had headed off to the Kulu Valley for a while.

Al had read the letter and left the Post Office, and walked up the street for about a hundred yards – he spotted Keith!

They greeted each other;

"Far out to see you again man," said Keith; "Where you been, I got here a few days after I left Amritsar – got kicked off the fucking train and had to hitch for bloody miles, ha! But here I am, how are you?"

Al replied: "What! I got kicked off a train too, in the middle of the jungle up between Haridwar and Rishikesh a couple of weeks ago. I had a ticket from Delhi to Haridwar but not to Rishikesh. It was only a couple of rupees but the bloody conductor wanted me to pay a hundred rupees fine – he pulled the emergency cord and stopped the train and made me get off. It was just jungle."

"Bloody hell man, at least they stopped at a station before I got the boot! What happened then – where you been since?", said Keith.

"Yeah, it turned out OK, I followed the railway track and then there was a road and a car stopped so I had a lift to Rishikesh and back to Haridwar with a great Indian family – they took me to see the Maharishi place, you know – the Transcendental meditation guru guy the Beatles had."

"Where you going next? I'm off to Nepal tomorrow, by bus, fuck the trains, man!" said Keith.

"God I've been really ill. I got dysentery and Infectious Hepatitis - I came back here and I was in Delhi hospital two weeks," explained Al. "I'm going to Amritsar in a couple of days, with Diane – this is Diane – this is Keith", introducing them.

Keith shook hands with Diane. "I've got to go get some stuff done – maybe we can meet up later, where you staying?"

"At a guest house called Mrs Colaca's on Janpath Lane – we got a room there – she's got about fifty cats! Come tonight, it's easy to find."

Keith had a map of New Delhi and Al showed him where the guest house was.

It was so hot that when Al drank tea or a fizzy drink, by the time he managed to cross the main road he was thirsty again. That was Delhi in September.

But Keith never showed up.

That evening, Al and Diane met a group of young English guys at the hostel. They had chatted for a while in the courtyard where there was a water pump that guests tended to gather round, covering themselves with cool water when the heat of the day had gotten too much.

One of the boys, Graham, was telling Al that they had come from England overland through Iran and Afghanistan. He had Hepatitis – he thought he had caught it in the opium den in Kabul!

Al said: "Wow, I went there and I got 'hep' too. I've been in hospital for two weeks I got dysentery too. They told me not to drink alcohol and not to eat fried food."

"Yep me too, we cook our own now – why don't you two come to eat with us tonight – just some boiled rice and boiled veggies – safer than eating round here, I think."

So, a couple of hours later, Al and Diane went to Graham's room. They smoked some joints with them, then Graham started pulling things out of his rucksack to get ready to cook. Al spotted a compass very similar to the one he had sold in Chicken Street in Kabul.

"Hey, I used to have a compass like that!" Al exclaimed, "I had to sell it in Kabul – funny thing was I got what it cost me in England, and the guy in the shop didn't seem to know what it was! I think he thought it was magic!"

Graham laughed out loud and said: "Bloody hell man, that's where I bought it, in a shop in Chicken Street. Yeh I don't think he knew what it was – weird innit – he kept showing me how it pointed up the street. How strange!"

Al looked more closely and, for sure, it looked exactly like the one he had sold.

Graham cooked a meal of green peppers stuffed with onions and carrots and rice. I knew Al thought it was delicious.

They ate with Graham the next day. They hardly went out of the hostel at all that day – it was well over one hundred degrees Fahrenheit. When they did go for a stroll round Connaught Circus, browsing the shops and trying to avoid the hawkers and the pools of red spat out by the Betel Nut chewers, suddenly the sky opened and it rained really heavily!

As Al and Diane darted into a shop for shelter, lots of Indian men and women ran out of the shops into the rain and started jumping for joy. So Al and Diane ran back into the rain, became soaked and joined the celebration. Apparently it was the first rain that year. The road became a little flooded and the traffic slowed, amidst a great honking of horns and ringing of bicycle rickshaw bells. It felt wonderful on my felt fabric.

The rain stopped as abruptly as it had started.

Al and Diane, now soaked, headed back to the hostel, but the heat had dried their clothing even before they got there.

Al looked out for Keith, but did not see him. The following day, July 14 1972, Al and Diane went first to the Iranian Embassy in Delhi to get a visa, then to the main railway station, which was about a mile from Connaught Circus, to buy tickets to Amritsar.

There was a queue of about fifty men at the one counter that seemed to be staffed and service was slow, even for India. Al and Diane queued for about half an hour and then they were approached by a well-dressed and middle-aged English lady.

"Excuse me," she said, "Do you know there is a lady's queue?"

"No," said Diane, "I can't see it, where is it?"

"Oh you can't see it my dear because there are so few women buying tickets, but you can go straight to the front of this queue and they will serve you next my dear."

So Al gave the money to Diane, and, sure enough, when she went to the counter the man serving went straight to her and she bought the tickets without having to wait at all.

Next day, they took a tuk-tuk – a three-wheeler motorised rickshaw – to the railway station, negotiated the crowds and found the correct platform and immediately boarded the train.

The train was just about to leave when Diane jumped up saying she needed to buy some food and water and rushed straight off the train, taking her bag with her, and ran down the platform.

Al waited a few minutes, and, as the train was obviously about to leave and Diane had not come back, he quickly hopped off the train and looked up and down the platform.

Diane was nowhere to be seen!

Al didn't know whether to wait in case she missed the train, or get on the train in case she had got back on into a different carriage.

The train started to pull away. As it began accelerating, Al decided all he could sensibly do was get back on – he spotted an open carriage door and ran and jumped aboard. An Indian voice said in English "Well done Sahib!"

Al found a seat and sat and enjoyed the journey but he discovered it was not possible to go from one carriage to another whilst the train was moving – unless, as some men seemed to do – he climbed out the door and onto the roof. He wasn't going to do that.

The train journey from Delhi to Amritsar was about two hundred and fifty miles and took over ten hours with several long stops at stations. By the time they arrived it was dark. There were plenty of Europeans and maybe Americans alighting from the train, but no sign of Diane. Al went directly to find free accommodation at the Golden Temple. It was signposted in English and a walk of about a mile.

After he found a bed in a room, he headed straight for the food hall. Inside, sitting with a small group of European travellers, was

145

Diane.

After dinner of rice and dahl with chapati, provided free to travellers by the Sikh Golden Temple donors, Al met with Diane and they agreed to try to catch a bus all the way to Rawalpindi in Pakistan. This would involve crossing the border but no visas were needed. Then in Rawalpindi they could go to nearby Islamabad to collect Diane's money and get visas for Afghanistan

The next day, July 20 1972, they met up and went to the bus station – there was a bus leaving that afternoon and it was due to arrive in Lahore in the evening. They would stay one night then get a bus to Rawalpindi. They bought tickets.

Al had been in India almost seven weeks.

A few hours later they were back at the bus station with their bags, had boarded the bus and were on their way to the border crossing at Attari – Wagah along the Grand Trunk Road. It was just about 20 miles and they arrived to be told that the bus would stop long enough to see the daily ceremonial lowering of flags at dusk.

This was one of the strangest military displays Al had ever seen. On each side or the border there were troops dressed in costumes and hats.

On the Indian side the troops wore black with black fan-like hats; on the Pakistani side they wore khaki with red fan hats.

It was like some sort of game, a flag-lowering with synchronised shouting and stamping of feet, with soldiers doing fast goose-step marches and high kicks with a waving of flags and shouting of orders – as if a show of one-upmanship – a battle of wits without bullets being fired with a great waving of arms, salutes and gestures. Crowds had gathered to watch this display. The gate was opened and closed and opened again, and the two country flags lowered simultaneously.

When the prancing and parading was over, Al and Diane walked through the customs and passport control and re-boarded the bus that took them towards Lahore.

Not long before they arrived, a young Pakistani man asked if they needed somewhere to stay. He had a house in a village just outside the city and they could stay for free.

Al and Diane agreed and got off the bus with the young man. He led them through a small village to a small house. They entered the house – it was completely devoid of furniture. Not even a chair or a bed.

The man explained that he had only just rented the house and was yet to move in, but if they waited then he would bring them blankets and a rug to sleep on and some tea and food. He left but did not come back.

Instead other young men started entering in groups of two and three, saying that they only wanted to speak in English, to practice for their school. They were all talking, about half a dozen with Al at one side of the front room, and others to Diane at the other side.

Suddenly Al heard Diane shouting – "No, get off of me, leave me alone!"

Al could see that Diane was looking very uncomfortable and up against the wall with about eight young guys in front of her. It reminded him of the similar situation in the Lahore film studio corridor with Miriam. But, he thought, that was in a public place, this is in a village.

He needed to act fast, so he did exactly what he had done before.

He pushed through the small crowd in front of him and crossed the room. He started shouting; "That is enough, stop it and go away!"

Some of the guys backed off.

He shouted again "Fuck off or I'll stab you!"

With that they started pointing at Diane and shouting at each other. Within a minute or so they had all left the house.

"Come on," said Al, "let's split before it gets dark and they come back."

As the light was fading, they walked back through the village to where the bus had stopped. People were shouting at them and it sounded like it may have been abuse. A woman threw a bucket of what looked like dirty water into the street in front of them.

"What's up with this fucking place?" asked Al.

"It's really aggressive here isn't it. Let's get into Lahore."

Just then a bus came along and they jumped aboard. Al knew exactly the place to stay, the Hotel Eden, where he had stayed with Keith a couple of months earlier. But the staff were different so he did not ask for Bhang, the cannabis drink that he had tried last time. So it wasn't long before they had eaten dinner and were in bed. Diane asked Al if he had brought any hash.

"No," he said, "Did you hear the tale about the customs woman there that is supposed to be psychic?"

A couple of days after arriving in Lahore, Diane told Al that she needed to go to the UK Embassy in Islamabad to collect the money that she hoped her parents had sent. They decided to go to Rawalpindi, a town connected to Islamabad and they would go by train.

So they went to the Lahore railway station and bought tickets to Rawalpindi, about a hundred and sixty miles, estimated to take five to six hours. The journey was uneventful, the views of no interest. They booked into a cheap hotel near the station.

On the following day, Al and Diane went together to Islamabad, a few miles away, to the embassy for Afghanistan to buy visas, and then Diane went alone to the UK Embassy to collect her money, whilst Al sat and ate one of the hottest dahl dishes he had ever eaten. It did cool him down though, it was about 100 degrees outside.

When Diane came back, she said she had to wait a few days.

Rawalpindi and Islamabad, although essentially two parts of one big city, were incredibly different. Rawalpindi consisted of old and dilapidated buildings. The streets were crowded and congested with an array of vehicles and people. It was all quite dirty.

On the other hand, Islamabad with its big hotels, embassies, Government buildings and business offices, seemed to have wider and cleaner streets, pavements to walk on, and was all-in-all seemingly more orderly if less pleasant than Rawalpindi.

So they stayed three days in Rawalpindi, which, despite the dirt, they enjoyed. They were able to buy some very cheap good black hash which they spent the days smoking on the hotel balcony, looking down onto the street and enjoying the view of the local life..

Diane went back to the Embassy and when she came back she was smiling – her money had arrived. And it was in English bank notes. She counted out just over one hundred pounds and gave half of it to Al. They decided to go straight to the bus station to get tickets to Peshawar the next day – a journey, they were told, of about four hours.

So they took the bus to Peshawar, stayed at the Paradise Hotel and bought tickets for a bus to Kabul the next day. Peshawar had not changed, it was still dirty and smelly.

The following day, July 29 1972, was the day of the bus ride back through the Khyber Pass to Kabul, the journey that had so impressed and inspired Al on his way to India a few months earlier.

They journeyed past trains of laden camels that occasionally blocked the road, fields with sheep and cattle, the strange-looking men wrapped in blankets even in the heat of the sun, standing or sitting is groups seemingly in the middle of nowhere.

There was an incredible movement of people across the border and back. Many were walking in groups. Many of the men were dressed in garments the light-brown colour of the earth. Others were dressed in coloured tunics with waistcoats over light trousers. Most wore turbans.

The women were dressed in colourful outfits or entirely in blue, black or coloured burkas and many carried large pots or bundles on their heads. The children waved at the bus.

The bus itself was a rickety old machine that chugged along up and down the hills. As well as Al and Diane, there were several other western-looking travellers – but sometimes it was hard to tell as they were tanned brown and dressed in clothes seen in India. In any case, they all kept themselves to themselves. There was no sign of any cannabis smoking.

As the road zig-zagged upwards, sometimes passing over bridges built over small streams, Al noticed the many tent cities below in the valley, all with herds of camels and donkeys. Higher were the remains of the many forts originally built by the British. In the distance were snowy peaks.

High on the pass were fortified buildings that were the homes of the locals, each with its own watchtower. In places the road had a simple and crude stone walls separating it from a sheer drop – in other places there was just the drop.

Then we arrived back in Kabul. Al and Diane headed straight for a small hotel in Chicken Street, called the Peace Hotel – Diane told Al that she had stayed there before and that it was cheap and had good food.

They had been there for about ten days when Al started to get sick again. I knew he was feeling worse each day, unable to eat or drink without being sick, until one day he realised that he could not stand straight without his head spinning and the feeling that he was about to black out.

He told Diane that he was going to a clinic and she found the address from reception and arranged for a taxi. Al left his bag but was sure to take his passport. Diane went with him to the hospital reception but did not stay – she took the same taxi back into the city.

Al had to wait about half an hour and then a doctor approached him, saying "Very sorry Sir, very few people here speak English – they had to fetch me from my home. It is a holiday for me today, but I come to see you."

He took Al into a room and asked his problem, which he explained briefly. The doctor called and a male nurse arrived and, without a word, took Al by the wrist and led him out of the room – as he left he spotted a poster that was warning against smallpox!

Al was led into a very large structure, the walls were made from corrugated-looking tin and the roof was canvas. It looked like it had well over one hundred big steel beds, most of them empty.

Al was led to a bed and given a bottle of water and the nurse gestured for him to stay. He got on the bed and instantly fell asleep.It was some time later that Al was awoken. The same male nurse took a sample of his blood.

A remarkably short time later, the nurse returned with a blood transfusion kit. They gave Al a pint of blood, into his arm, and when that was done, several pints of plasma. The nurse motioned to Al so he understood to drink water. Al just kept dozing off. Several times somebody woke him and gave him sugarless black tea, then the evening meal arrived. It was rice. Just soggy white rice. But Al was hungry and ate it all.

It was two days before Diane arrived for a visit. She had waited, she said, for Al to come back, then tried unsuccessfully to phone the hospital for information, then decided to get a taxi.

Al spoke to somebody for the first time in two days. Diane told him that the taxi-driver had helped her find him and that he had translated for her – Al had been at such a point of dehydration that his life was at risk. She said that the doctor here had said there was nobody else who to spoke English but in another two or three days an English-speaking doctor would come and until then, Al had to stay!

True to that, the English-speaking doctor that Al had first met at reception, appeared three days later.

Al had been there for five days.The doctor said that he was surprised that Al was still there; he should have been there for just one day but nobody knew. He said Al could go now.

Al then realised that he did not have any money and told the doctor – his money was at the hotel. The doctor gave Al some few Afghani notes and told him that he could get a bus outside that would take him to the city centre. From there a short walk took him back to the Peace Hotel in Chicken Street.

Diane was there. She was not happy. She told Al how she had met an English woman whose husband had been in prison for drugs for two years and she had given her most of her money. The she said "And I've lost my passport!"

"Oh no, how did that happen? Are you getting a new one?"

"I don't know," she said, "It was in my bag and then it was gone. I went to the embassy and they are getting me a new one in about a week, they just gave me a temporary document for ID in case I need it. They told the police. I've got to go back in a week."

"Wow, that's not too good, we've got to get out of here next week, our visa's run out and I've not got much money left!" said Al.

"I've got none either, well not much," said Diane.

"Bloody hell that all went quick!"

"And," she continued, "When I get a new passport I've got to go back to the border to get an entry stamp, then

we got to get our visas extended."

"Well that's not too bad – it was a brilliant bus ride, I don't mind, I'll come with you. Got to get some money too, somehow."

"I'm not going to go back to the border," said Diane,.

"I don't see why I should, it's obvious I'm here so I must have come into the bloody place – they can stuff it. I'll get my passport but I am not going back."

Al decided not to argue. He just explained that it was all formality and if Diane wanted to cross into Iran she would need an entry visa and it was only at the Pakistan border that they probably have a record of when they had come in.

That didn't work.

Diane said rather loudly: "Look, I'm not going back, right. They can phone up or do it in the post I don't care. It's just stupid."

"Well anyway," said Al, "we've got to get some money or I'm going to die here. I don't have much energy. I'm going to go to the embassy and see a if they will lend me some money or something. I've got bank account but there's no money in it, maybe they will give me an overdraft.

"I reckon if I can get one hundred pounds, it will get us both home.

" If we can get to Istanbul, I know the Pudding Shop – we may be able to get a cheap lift to UK or Germany or somewhere from there - they have a noticeboard where people can ask for a ride.

"I'll do that tomorrow – might get some money before you get your passport – I've got enough to last a while, it's cheap here.

"Here, you better have some."

He counted out some notes that were part of what he had left out of what Diane had given him. It was ten pounds.

"Don't give it away," he said.

That evening they went to Sigis just down Chicken Street, sat and ate, chatted with other travellers, some going one way and some going the other, drank milkshakes and smoked joints. All for less than one pound.

The following day Al went to the embassy for the UK. He was sent in to see an English official who asked lots of questions. Then he said that the embassy could not contact a bank and asked was there anyone that Al could ask for funds to be sent, what about his parents, where did they live?

Al provided the information. The official said it would take about a week but if there was no other way, they could not give Al a loan, but they could fly him back to the UK.

Al told him about Diane. The official said that when she got her passport and entry visa stamped into it, she should come to see him – or she could come in sooner – they would have to see her before he could say how they could help.

Al went back to meet Diane at Sigis and told her what was happening.

"I'm still not going back to the border though," she said.

They had lunch and smoked a couple of joints of hash. Suddenly Diane said "Hey, you want some of these?"

She held out her hand and in her palm were four or so small squares of blank paper.

"What's that?" asked Al "looks like paper!" he laughed.

"It's acid," she said, "LSD, you know, Lucy in the Sky. I got some from a French guy. He reckoned they're really good! Want to try?"

Al found her manner too seductive to resist.

"How many do we take? How strong are they? How long do they last? I've never done it."

"I don't know," she said "I've got four. You take two and I'll take two."

"I think I'll just take one first time," he said.

With that Diane popped one small square of paper into Al's mouth. "Suck it and see," she laughed.

Al laughed and then frowned as he watched Diane put the other three squares into her own mouth.

She washed it down with a fizzy drink.

"So this is going to be a trip", thought Al.

He thought about the books he had read – "Aldous Huxley and

Timothy Leary, about LSD and other psychedelic drugs: there was that book by the guy that gave acid to dolphins and then took it himself and put himself into an "isolation tank" and had met beings made out of light. What was his name? Oh yeah, John Lily's Eye of the Cyclone. Oh and the Carlos Castaneda's tales about a Shaman that took psychedelic plants to make contact with beings on other levels.

"The Beatles of course – was that before or after they had gone to Rishikesh with the Maharishi Mahesh Yogi?

"The whole hippy thing was a lot to do with LSD and love and peace and flowers, so that is obviously what it's about – a good time, a spiritual time – just probably stronger than hash."

He looked up from his thoughts and started to look around the courtyard.

It looked different!

Al thought that he hadn't noticed the bells hanging from the edge of the roof, or the bright red flowerpots that held the small trees. And there seemed to be more flowers than before. Yet he'd been there several times before.

Some of the people there, the Westerners, started to look quite funny the way they were dressed. Bandanna's! He hadn't noticed them – in Kabul – they looked really out of place!

Funny how so many were wearing blue jeans, including the two guys serving – and they had short hair, the customers all had long hair.

Weird that people came here to Sigis to eat food they could get back home.

Some of the people looked like people Al had known, or like mixtures of two of them. Several times he felt like shouting out to them, but then they moved and turned into themselves again. How strange, how funny.

He started to laugh and turned to Diane to tell her his thoughts – she was looking at a colourful bird, some sort of canary, that was standing on on top of a small green shrub, almost motionless, as she was. She looked mesmerised, so Al kept quiet, laughing again in his head.

Al turned back to look at the people again.

That guy looked familiar.

As he looked at the guy, the guy stood up and walked over.

"Hi!", he said. "Are you Al?"

Al felt a little uneasy at that – how did the guy know his name?

"You from Norwich? I'm Pete – remember me – Pete Roscoe?"

"Wow," said Al, "You are Pete Roscoe, yeah, I remember you of course, I thought you were somebody that looked like him, I mean you!", he laughed.

Al had known Pete Roscoe back in Norwich but had had no idea that he too, would be heading for India. Pete had also known John and Keith.

"How you doing man?" said Pete, "How long you been here, where you going? "

Al answered: "I went to India with Keith and then I got sick – Infectious Hepatitis and dysentery, nearly died, had no money, on my own, in Haridwar in the Northern Foothills. But I got to hospital in Delhi – I've been in hospital here too. Just waiting to get some money to get home. I'm with Diane. I want to get her home too."

He turned to introduce Pete to Diane. She was staring into a glass of fizzy drink and quietly giggling.

"Hi Pete!"

Al knew that Pete had known John and maybe Mike, so he asked Pete: "Have you heard anything about John and Mike? Keith and I left them with the van in Antalya in Turkey and caught a boat to Iskenderun – we hitched from there across Syria to Baghdad. I haven't heard from them – we were supposed to meet them back in Istanbul but decided to carry on to India. Are they back in

England yet?"

"God what a drag about John – you don't know what happened, do you?" asked Pete.

"No," said Al.

"Wow man, I hate to tell you this," said Pete, "John was killed in a crash the night you left them in Turkey. Mike had broken his two legs and some ribs and was in hospital there for several weeks. I heard they crashed into a parked truck on a bend at night – John was driving – he swerved out and probably saved Mike's life, but was killed himself. Everyone was real sick about it, man."

It may have been because Al was still in some doubt that this was actually Pete Roscoe – maybe that cushioned the blow for him – he was tripping on acid and just been told his best friend John had died hours after he had last seen him.

So Pete and Al chatted a while longer, Pete was on his way to India. Al gave him some advice about being really careful about what he ate and drank, to keep hydrated, and not to drink the Ganges.

Then it was time that Pete said he would have to go as he had people to meet. They agreed to meet in the same place at lunch time the next day.

Al ordered another two teas with milk. It tasted weird. Different. He didn't drink his.

Then he felt it time to go and explore the streets.

"Come on Diane, let's go for a walkabout. I want some of those spicy potatoes and corn on the cob I've seen."

So they went outside to see the street.

"Where are we?" asked Diane.

"Sigis, Chicken Street!" said Al.

"Or is it? Hang on, it's not Chicken Street, we must have come out of a different door!" exclaimed Al – "Wait a minute, there's that Kabul restaurant place – it is Chicken Street – wow, it looks different, I never noticed all those ribbons and flags – hey be careful where you walk, there's holes all over the place – hey look at that donkey, it's only got three legs!"

"Hey this is great, let's go look at Flower Street!"

"Okay," said Diane. She wasn't saying much but she had a big grin. She took hold of Al's arm.

"Don't let me fall down a hole, it's really tricky up here with the wind," she said.

Al couldn't feel any wind and we were not high up at all, from the road – well I guess if we're 6,000 feet above sea level we must be "up here".

"Six thousand feet and climbing!" he said for no real reason.

So they strolled down Chicken Street towards Flower Street, looking in the shop windows and at stalls that Al thought he had never seen before. Everything except the road itself was much more colourful and shiny than he remembered, except the road had many massive piles of dung on it. As he looked, he saw a donkey adding more to it!

All the local merchants seemed to be nodding and smiling at them today! Al thought they all looked like – well they were on something - they were tripping too! Well, thought Al, I guess you've got to be on something to live here – it's like magic.

They reached the end of Chicken Street where it joined Flower Street.

It looked really busy with people that obviously weren't tripping.. It didn't look magic at all. Dark and damp with too many hidden spots, thought Al. Despite the flowers it was not inviting. Noisy too. Chicken Street had seemed very quiet – probably all the shoppers were down here.

"Let's go back – or down by the river, we could see the Mosque," he said.

"Yeah let's go that way, to the Mosque," laughed Diana. "It doesn't matter where we land, we'll be OK."

It seemed like hours before they reached the Mosque and Al had to sit down.

He sat on a low wall outside a building where he could see the Mosque and got lost in thoughts about the good and bad of religions and how the bad side made it hard to believe, yet so many had fallen for religions, as if it was some sort of spell to control people. Al did not want to be a part of religion – he wanted to be apart from them all. "If there's a God," he thought, "it's not in religion."

He heard Diane shouting "Get off, go away, Help!"

He turned to see Diane standing on the wall and below her were three dogs. They were jumping up at her in a friendly way, thought Al.

"It's OK, they're just trying to be friendly, just get down and pet them!"

"No they're trying to bite me, they won't leave me alone. They might have rabies!"

"But they're only little," said Al.

"No they're not, they're massive. They're not dogs – they're wolves. Help! Please!" She was really freaked.

Al just shooed the dogs away. They went off down the street, stopped and looked back. Al shouted "Go!" Off they went, hunting for food probably.

He helped Diane climb down. She hugged him.

"Well obviously, cos she took three, she's right out of it", thought Al.

He grabbed her by the arm and they went back to Sigis where they could relax in a good friendly atmosphere and listen to some good rock music.

"Kabul streets at night", he said, "Not good on acid!"

That was a good decision. Diane calmed down and they both enjoyed the rest of the trip, going back to the Peace Hotel with a nice piece of hash to smoke, until they dozed off as dawn was breaking and the Mullahs were calling the so-called faithful to prayer, from their minaret towers.

The following day, Al went back to Sigis and, sure enough, Pete Roscoe was there. It was the real Pete and they chatted a while about what they had been through and, of course, the devastating news about John and Mike. Pete said everyone was really worried about Al as news had reached Norwich that he had been ill.

Diane gave Al a book, called the I Ching. He had in fact seen it before - Keith had shown him the book in Norwich before they had left. It was the 'Book of Changes', an oracle, not so much a fortune teller, more of a clarifier. Al learned from Diane that by throwing three coins six times and recording the results, one could "ask" the book a question, for advice, and the coins would reveal a set of lines that led to readings.

And so the days passed, pretty much day to day, up and down Chicken Street, getting high, meeting people, eating western foods and waiting. No more acid though!

Then came the day that Diane was given her replacement passport – now she just needed the entry visa. That same day in the morning there was a message at reception for Al to go back to the embassy.

Off he went – "things are working out," he thought. He took a taxi to the embassy, just to be positive. Al arrived at the embassy and was shown in to the office he had been in previously and met the same embassy official.

The guy told Al that the authorities had been in touch with Al's parents and they had sent some money – One hundred and seventy pounds – enough for a flight back to London and some change.

"Well," thought Al, "that's about six weeks wages for Dad."

Then he thought: "Well God, if you are there, please let them be able to afford that, not let them get into debt." (I can tell you now as it seems the best time, but Al did not know for weeks afterwards, that round about that time they had had a small win on the "football pools" whatever that is – it as in fact as if his prayer had been answered.)

Al told the embassy chap that he did not want to spend all that money getting home and agreed to take seventy pounds in cash – English money - and leave the rest at the embassy.

"That way," he said, "I can get home and get my friend Diane home too."

He took the money and arranged that he could get the rest transferred to any country on route or get it refunded to his parents.

He already had his visa, Diane had her passport, all that was needed was to make the return bus ride to the border. He went back to meet Diane at Sigis restaurant, that had become their regular haunt. They would go for a "slap-up" meal.

After a milk shake and a smoke, Al found the name of a good restaurant and took Diane for a big meal. Well, it ended up that the only vegetarian food available in this top restaurant in a big hotel, was Kabuli rice with vegetables on the side, yoghurt, bread and fruit. They could have eaten exactly the same in a local cheap restaurant for a fifth of the price and in a better atmosphere.

Al said to Diane, "So tomorrow morning we can get the bus to the border and back and sort out your visa, then we can get tickets and head back across Iran. It'll be fun."

"I've told you loads of times, don't you listen," she said, "I'm not going, it's stupid, they know I am here – if they say I can't get out of the country without a stamp to say I came in, that's just daft! So what I can't even fly out – what about if they wanted to kick me out, they'd soon do that. End of!"

The following morning, Al got himself up and when he woke Diane, told her if she wanted to go to the border today, get up and go with him.

Diane refused. They had a noisy row.

Al realised that she was not going to cooperate.

Al turned to his I Ching and, throwing three Afghani coins, asked "What should I do - stay with Diane or make the journey home alone?"

It seemed very sound and clear advice - from the book - that he had to make the journey home - the alternative suggested led to disaster.

Later that day he told Diane "Tomorrow I am getting up and going to the bus station. If you want to come, we will go to the border. I not, I'm going to catch a bus to Herat

"Look, here is half my money that's left, thirty pounds," handing her the English notes and a few Afghani notes.

"So it's up to you. Fifty pounds should get us both back to London if we share."

"Thanks," she said, "Maybe I'll see you in England one day. I'm not going to the Pakistan border and if they aren't going to let me out to Iran, I'll have to stay here."

Al struggled but he could not understand why she was being so stubborn, it was only a bus ride.

"If I stay here I am going to die," he said.

After that they did not talk about it and drifted back to a day at Sigis getting high.

The following morning, fighting with his conscience, finding that Diane was not going to join him, Al left. He went straight to the bus station and caught a bus to Herat, via Kandahar. It was normal for the bus to stop one night at Kandahar and he would sleep on the bus.

In that way he arrived in Herat the following day, spent one night there, bought a ticket to the border and from there a ticket all the way to Tehran.

Al crossed the border at Islam Qala and on to the Iranian side at Tayebad on September 3, 1972. He had been in Afghanistan this time for 40 days and 40 nights.

It was about fifteen hundred miles from Kabul to Tehran, Mashhad being about half way.

By the time he reached Tehran, he felt filthy dirty not having washed properly for four or five days. He was very tired and very hungry and thirsty. He found a small hotel near the bus station, booked a room for one and before long was asleep

The following morning, Al awoke and had a good breakfast at a small café. He decided to head off to the American Express offices to see if they could get any money that was waiting for him in Delhi sent to him that day in Tehran. Then, he planned, he would organise transport somehow to Istanbul. From there he would seek a lift closer to the UK at the Pudding Shop.

He thought a lot about Diane, hoping she was OK, but that was her choice. Al believed in freedom of choice. "Well," he thought, "She was penniless when he had first met her in Delhi, now at least she had money and a passport again – and if she hangs about at Sigis she'll probably get a lift. She'll be OK, she's a survivor and it wasn't her that was dying from dysentery and Infectious Hepatitis."

He was given directions to the American Express Offices, left his bag in the room and with me upon his head, started to walk the busy streets.

But it was getting hotter and hotter. Al was feeling weaker and weaker – he had to sit down.

The only place to sit was on the dirty pavement.

He must have looked terrible. His long hair and his clothing was dirty. He was very thin – it turned out that he had lost about a third of his body weight, now being a little over ninety pounds.

He sat there a while. The street was crowded, the road full of traffic, as usual a great honking of horns as cars, taxis, buses and trucks fought to some space to drive into. The traffic was very slow.

Nobody seemed to care about Al – he thought about the 'Good Samaritan' story in the New Testament – would there be one here?

He tried to stand up and almost fainted. He tried getting the attention of a passer-by for ages, to no avail. Then, when he had stopped trying to get help, it came in the form of a young guy, probably Iranian, in jeans and shirt.

The chap asked Al if he was OK. "No, I am not and thanks for stopping – I think I have to go to the British Embassy, do you know where it is please?" asked Al.

"Sorry my friend, I do not know, but the American Embassy is around the next corner and you will see it, not far my friend, I will show you" said the guy and with that helped Al stand up and took him to the street and pointed.

"There is US Embassy," he said, pointing. But what Al saw was the Union Jack, the British flag! It was the UK Embassy building after all.

Al said thanks and goodbye and headed down the street, crossing over and going in through what looked like an entrance. At the gate stood a large security guard in some sort of ceremonial costume. As Al approached the guard said "Embassy closed today!"

"I'm British," said Al, "I am ill, you cannot stop me coming on to British soil can you? I want to see somebody for help."

"You can go inside but there is nobody here to see you today – come back tomorrow, Sir," stressed the guard.

So Al walked in, the guard following, saying again, "Come back tomorrow". Al saw a wooden door and it opened so he went in.

Inside was a large room with wooden tables and chairs, some wooden benches by the wall, and at the far end what looked like a reception office with a closed shutter. He headed for a bench and lay on it.

"I will wait here until somebody comes and please bring me some good water to drink."

The guard went off and a few minutes later he came back with two sealed glass bottles full of water. Al drank almost a whole bottle, lay down again on the wooden bench and fell asleep.

Some time later, probably several hours, an embassy official arrived.

He seemed a pleasant and sympathetic chap and Al explained his situation.

"Well, you can't stay here – I think we should get you to the hospital so they can do some tests!"

Al agreed and the official led him out to a car and took him a few miles to the outskirts of Tehran where the hospital was.

Once inside the hospital, the embassy official stayed until an English-speaking doctor came and Al had explained his problems. Then he left saying that he would stay in touch.

The doctor said Al should stay at least one night and they would do tests. He took Al's pulse and blood pressure, listened through his stethoscope at Al's chest, pressed on his abdomen and took a sample of blood.

Al was then told to lay on a bed trolley and with me in his hand, was taken to a small ward and led to a bed. Of course he did not have clothing to change into, but they brought him some over-sized pyjamas. They also brought Al a hot meal but it had meat in it. Al explained that he did not eat flesh and, although he felt that the nurse really did not understand either what he was saying or why he did not eat meat, the meal was soon replaced with rice and vegetables and no meat. It was delicious and felt wholesome.

Al was shown where the wash room with shower was and quickly stripped off, washed his body and hair and washed his clothes all at the same time. He did not wash me though. I think I needed it to rain, I was dirty too.

He went back to his bed. He was feeling a lot better now. He fell asleep. I was on a small cabinet next to his bed, next to some bottles of water and a small vase with flowers in!

Some time later, a male nurse woke Al up and handed his some tablets, which he swallowed. He went back to sleep.

It was the following morning that he awoke. They served him a breakfast of some sort of porridge, eggs and bread, yoghurt and a rice pudding.

The doctor came and explained to Al that they had the results of the tests and that he should stay a few nights and take the tablets.

"When you go it is very important – you must not drink alcohol and you must not eat fried food or fresh fruit or salad."

Later that day the embassy official came to visit Al. He told Al that the best action for him was to take a flight home. Al explained his lack of money but that he had money in Kabul and maybe some at the American Express if he could get it sent from Delhi offices.

The guy left and came back about an hour later.

He said that if Al signed a paper giving authority, the embassy could arrange with the embassy in Kabul and the American Express in Delhi. Al could stay at the hospital another four nights and then the Embassy would arrange for a car to pick him up and he would be able to fly to London.

Al told him yes but his bag was at the hotel and he had to pay the extra bill.

So the official said "OK, we will pick you up by car and take you to your hotel, you stay only for one night, OK? Then we take you to the airport."

Al agreed. That was the last he saw of the official. But for four more days and nights he felt warm and clean and was well fed and medicated.

On the final morning, sure enough, a car from the embassy arrived and took AL first to the American Express where he picked up just twenty pounds that had been sent to Delhi and then he headed back to the hotel. He paid his bill.

After a small outing to a nearby restaurant where he ate vegetables and rice again, he went back to his hotel feeling very tired as if it had been a hard day, and soon again he was asleep.

After breakfast next day, Al went out and bought some limes as he had been told they were good to fight Infectious Hepatitis.

Soon enough, the car arrived again and Al was taken to Tehran airport and given his ticket for a flight to London Heathrow airport. He asked the driver to ask the embassy to phone his parents to tell them he was due to arrive, writing down the phone number.

Al put me into his rucksack and that was all I knew until we landed.

Al had to go through customs at Heathrow Airport. They opened his rucksack and there I was, soon to be back on Al's head and back in communication.

Next to come out was Al's worn and dirty sleeping bag – but as it was being pulled out, about half a dozen limes came with it, falling to the ground and rolling down the slightly inclined floor. The customs officer quickly caught them and put them back into the rucksack saying "Thank you, you can go!"

Al found a phone box and phoned his parents in Wales, telling them he would catch a train to Cardiff and then a bus.

Al's mother said "We'll pick you up in Cardiff – we have a little car now and your Dad is driving. We had a little win on the pools just after we heard you were ill and that was how we got the money so quick."

"Prayers do get answered," thought Al to himself.

When his parents met Al on Cardiff General railway station, his Dad said "You look like Gandhi – you are so thin."

Back in Wales, the following day, the family doctor visited and said that Al would have to go to hospital and stay in for a while and have tests to see what was wrong. Al explained that he was on tablets from the hospital in Iran and that he was diagnosed with Infectious Hepatitis and dysentery. The doctor asked to see the pills.

"I'll keep them, you don't need them and we don't know what they are. They may not be good for you if they are from Iran! We'll get the tests done and find out the problem."

So Al was taken to a hospital near Cardiff. He had written some letters to friends in Norwich, such as Pam and also to Australian Paul, as well as John's parents saying how sorry he was to hear the sad news about his death - and Al asked his Mum to post them. As he was leaving his parents house, he picked me off the hook I had been on, saying "Mustn't forget Myhat, my old travelling buddy."

Al explained to the doctors that he was vegetarian and had been told not to eat fried food, fruit or salads. The doctor said "We'll see when we've done the tests"

They fed him on salad and chips!

Al's Mum visited every day, and one day she came again, with some letters from Norwich and a newspaper.

One letter was from two good friends, Pam and Steve, saying that he could stay with them when Al got back to Norwich and saying how sad they had been to hear that John was dead."

John had been a very much loved man and admired man by so many. Everyone that knew his was devastated at the news, they wrote.

But 'Stay away from Paul, he's taken up some sort of Guru called Maharaji', they wrote.

The second letter was from Paul, saying how he had given up

drugs and was meditating on something called "Knowledge" that he had been shown by a boy just fifteen years of age called Guru Maharaji.

There was another letter too, from John's parents, wishing Al well and saying "John died amongst the people he loved so much.Al finished reading the letter and picked up the newspaper. He opened it randomly and there in front of him was an article about the "Boy wonder Guru Maharaji" that had come from Haridwar in India, an ashram called Prem Nagar, to bring his "Knowledge" to the West. There was a small picture with a caption that read "Lord of the Universe".

"How strange," thought Al - "that must be the place opposite where I nearly drowned in the Ganges – I wonder if that is some sort of child prodigy for that Maharishi Yogi guru guy that the Beatles had seen – but that was called Transcendental Meditation and now this is called Knowledge."

A couple of days later, the test results were through and sure enough he had Infectious Hepatitis and dysentery – they gave Al pills and a strict diet of no alcohol, no fried food and no fresh fruit or salad.

He went home and stayed with his parents for several weeks, putting on weight and rebuilding his strength. I stayed on a hook by the front door.

Later Al put me into a special box.

The next thing I knew, I was in Norwich.

Al was staying with his two good friends, Pam and Steve, and visiting Australian Paul and his wife - there were no more chillums and joints with Paul. Instead, Paul told Al much about his boy teacher, the Guru Maharaji, and the techniques that the boy gave to enable people to experience the "Knowledge" within inside themselves.

Al was now actively seeking some sort of answer to an uncertain question about life and the universe. He started asking the I Ching – the book that Diane had given him in Kabul - for guidance.

One day whilst Al was about to consult the I Ching again, having thrown the coins and drawn the lines that would produce the reading, there was a knock on the door.

It was Australian Paul and Lorraine and another follower of the Guru Maharaji calles Alastair.

Al did not want to be unsociable, so made tea, and then whilst the three guests chatted away, telling him once again about this "Knowledge", all could not resist picking up the book again.

The 'lines' pointed him to read Hexagram 5 – "The Waiting", as he wished that Paul would stop talking so that he could focus on the reading, Al reached the lines that read:

"Six at the top means:

"One falls into the pit.

"Three uninvited guests arrive.

"Honour them, and in the end there will be good fortune."

It did not take Al long to realise that the three uninvited guests may well have been sitting in his living room.

So he started listening and began to understand that Paul was talking about some sort of experience within a person - an experience that he called peace.

Al started going to public meetings about this Knowledge – the meetings were called "Satsang" - he learnt that it was free for the asking but took commitment – "to yourself," the Guru said.

One day Al picked up his I Ching again and asked "Who is Guru Maharaji?"

The result was the revelation of Hexagram 1 "The Creative" changing to Hexagram 50: "The Cauldron" with changing lines in positions first and fifth.

Al was determined to find out – but that is another story.

I can tell you now, that Al never saw Mike, Miriam, Hellmut or Diane again and never went back to Turkey, Syria, Iraq, Iran or Pakistan. He wonders to this day where those people that he met are today and whether they were still alive.

I have since travelled with Al on many occasions and I have more adventurous tales to tell you about.

Until then, Peace be upon you. Myhat.

READERS' COMMENTS

Ann C, Norwich: "This is a fascinatng book packed with stories about adventures on the "Hippy Trail" in all its reality.It was harsh with extreme discomfort.heat and dust and sometimes illness. It took strength and endurance .but then. the rewards were a rich awareness of other cultures and beliefs. I recommend it warmly.and did I mention, it is so funny!"

Roger W E, Swansea: "My Hat is becoming an independent friend, as I read on - he/she/it is competing with you! Roger WE"

Chris P, Essex: "Awesome read fella, most enjoyable."

Ian L, Norfolk: "Read it before Christmas, liked it, very entertaining, definitely a good read, well done Alun."

Frank K, W Sussex: "Loved the book Alun and have shown friends, also travellers with a Hippie hat. Great days to remember for you I bet. I like the way you laid out the text too, great read."

Mark S, Norfolk: "Loving the book."

Melissa D, Italy "I really enjoyed this book..... but I have to admit I skipped some of the travel book descriptions. My favourite part is..... No, I won't spoil it for you!

16347181R00098

Printed in Poland
by Amazon Fulfillment
Poland Sp. z o.o., Wrocław